David Hammons
Bliz-aard Ball Sale

Elena Filipovic

AF754677

One Work Series Editor
Mark Lewis

Editor
Caroline Woodley

Assistant Editor
Louis Hartnoll

Copy Editor
Deirdre O'Dwyer

Editorial Assistant
Bo Choy

Afterall
Central Saint Martins
University of the Arts London
Granary Building
1 Granary Square
London N1C 4AA
www.afterall.org

Afterall is a Research Centre of
University of the Arts London

Directors
Charles Esche, Mark Lewis

This publication is made possible in part through a grant from the Barr Ferree Foundation Fund for Publications, Department of Art and Archaeology, Princeton University and through a Creative Capital | Warhol Foundation Arts Writers Grant

Design
Andrew Brash

Original design
A2/SW/HK
Typefaces
A2/SW/HK + A2-Type

Printed and bound by
die Keure, Belgium

The *One Work* series is printed on FSC-certified papers

ISBN 978-1-84638-186-7

Distribution by The MIT Press,
Cambridge, Massachusetts and London
www.mitpress.mit.edu

First published in 2017 by Afterall Books.
This third edition published in 2022

© 2022 Afterall, Central Saint Martins, University of the Arts London, the artists and the authors

All images of works by David Hammons
© 2022 the artists and the photographers

Supported using public funding by
ARTS COUNCIL ENGLAND

ual: central saint martins

An Afterall Book
Distributed by The MIT Press

Each book in the *One Work* series presents a single work of art considered in detail by a single author. The focus of the series is on contemporary art and its aim is to provoke debate about significant moments in art's recent development.

Over the course of more than one hundred books, important works will be presented in a meticulous and generous manner by writers who believe passionately in the originality and significance of the works about which they have chosen to write. Each book contains a comprehensive and detailed formal description of the work, followed by a critical mapping of the aesthetic and cultural context in which it was made and that it has gone on to shape. The changing presentation and reception of the work throughout its existence is also discussed, and each writer stakes a claim on the influence 'their' work has on the making and understanding of other works of art.

The books insist that a single contemporary work of art (in all of its different manifestations), through a unique and radical aesthetic articulation or invention, can affect our understanding of art in general. More than that, these books suggest that a single work of art can literally transform, however modestly, the way we look at and understand the world. In this sense the *One Work* series, while by no means exhaustive, will eventually become a veritable library of works of art that have made a difference.

Other titles in the *One Work* series:

Bas Jan Ader: In Search of the Miraculous
by Jan Verwoert

Hollis Frampton: (nostalgia)
by Rachel Moore

Ilya Kabakov: The Man Who Flew into Space from his Apartment
by Boris Groys

Richard Prince: Untitled (couple)
by Michael Newman

Joan Jonas: I Want to Live in the Country (And Other Romances)
by Susan Morgan

Mary Heilmann: Save the Last Dance for Me
by Terry R. Myers

Marc Camille Chaimowicz: Celebration? Realife
by Tom Holert

Yvonne Rainer: The Mind is a Muscle
by Catherine Wood

Fischli and Weiss: The Way Things Go
by Jeremy Millar

Andy Warhol: Blow Job
by Peter Gidal

Alighiero e Boetti: Mappa
by Luca Cerizza

Chris Marker: La Jetée
by Janet Harbord

Hanne Darboven: Cultural History 1880—1983
by Dan Adler

Michael Snow: Wavelength
by Elizabeth Legge

Sarah Lucas: Au Naturel
by Amna Malik

Richard Long: A Line Made by Walking
by Dieter Roelstraete

Marcel Duchamp: Étant donnés
by Julian Jason Haladyn

General Idea: Imagevirus
by Gregg Bordowitz

Dara Birnbaum: Technology/Transformation: Wonder Woman
by T.J. Demos

Gordon Matta-Clark: Conical Intersect
by Bruce Jenkins

Jeff Wall: Picture for Women
by David Campany

Jeff Koons: One Ball Total Equilibrium Tank
by Michael Archer

Richard Hamilton: Swingeing London 67 (f)
by Andrew Wilson

Martha Rosler: The Bowery in two inadequate descriptive systems
by Steve Edwards

Dan Graham: Rock My Religion
by Kodwo Eshun

Yayoi Kusama: Infinity Mirror Room — Phalli's Field
by Jo Applin

Michael Asher: Kunsthalle Bern, 1992
by Anne Rorimer

Sanja Iveković: Triangle
by Ruth Noack

Hélio Oiticica and Neville D'Almeida: Block-Experiments in Cosmococa — program in progress
by Sabeth Buchmann and Max Jorge Hinderer Cruz

Rodney Graham: Phonokinetoscope
by Shepherd Steiner

Philip Guston: The Studio
by Craig Burnett

Lee Lozano: Dropout Piece
by Sarah Lehrer-Graiwer

Thomas Hirschhorn: Deleuze Monument
by Anna Dezeuze

Mike Kelley: Educational Complex
by John Miller

Lee Friedlander: The Little Screens
by Saul Anton

Sturtevant: Warhol Marilyn
by Patricia Lee

Agnes Martin: Night Sea
by Suzanne Hudson

Sigmar Polke: Girlfriends
by Stefan Gronert

Glenn Ligon: Untitled (I Am a Man)
by Gregg Bordowitz

Walker Evans: Kitchen Corner
by Olivier Richon

David Hammons
Bliz-aard Ball Sale

Elena Filipovic

First and foremost, I would like to thank David Hammons, who inspired and for many years skirted this enquiry. It is to his lifetime of percussive work that this book pays homage, and it is through his ever elusive but generous spirit that his story could be chased and this book could find its form.

I am also tremendously grateful to Dawoud Bey, Linda Goode Bryant, A.C. Hudgins, the late Jack Tilton and Angela Valeria, each of whom was instrumental at key moments of my research. Throughout, Alhena Katsof was my most precious companion on the project, not only tirelessly assisting me with research but also interviewing on my behalf many of the individuals whose testimonies give this book its particular voice – and wings.

For so graciously sharing their stories, I thank Marina Adams, Jules Allen, Candida Alvarez, Dawoud Bey, Camille Billops, Horace Brockington, Steve Cannon, Janine Cirincione, Gylbert Coker, Papo Colo, C. Daniel "Danny" Dawson, Norman Douglas, Erma Estwick, the late John Farris, Tom Finkelpearl, Linda Goode Bryant, Jeanne Greenberg Rohatyn, Alex Harsley, James Hatch, Janet Henry, A.C. Hudgins, Suzanne Jackson, Arthur Jafa, Corinne Jennings, Kerry James Marshall, Barbara McCullough, Senga Nengudi, Joe Overstreet, Sandra Payne, Sara Penn, Vernon Reid, Adam Sheffer, Coreen Simpson, Frank Stewart, Bruce Talamon, Greg Tate, Robert Farris Thompson, Henry Threadgill, Guy Trebay, Angela Valeria, Faythe Weaver, Brian Wolff, Judith Wolff and Stanley Whitney. I also thank Emiliano Battista, Xena G. Becker, Philip Brookman, Abraham Cruzvillegas, Pradeep Dalal, Meredith Dunn, Susan Fensten, Hal Foster, Carmen Hammons, Lauren Hudgins, Thomas J. Lax, Susan L. Lehre, Dirk Pauwels, Iolanda Pensa, Lois Plehn, David Senior, Robert Sill and Connie Tilton for their help at different stages of the process.

No such study would be possible without the pioneering work of Kellie Jones. I am grateful as well to Thelma Golden, Glenn Ligon and Fred Moten for the models that they offered through their work, which informed so much of my thinking here. A number of extraordinary photographers – Dawoud Bey, Erma Estwick, Coreen Simpson, Frank Stewart and Bruce Talamon – helped make it possible for Hammons's work to be well represented here. Antonia Hirsch, Tom McDonough and Senam Okudzeto kindly read versions of this draft; many of their generous comments fed their way into the final manuscript. Finally, I gratefully acknowledge

Creative Capital | The Andy Warhol Foundation, which provided an Arts Writers Grant at a crucial moment, making much of the research and writing of this book possible, and Princeton University's Barr Ferree Foundation Publication Fund, for helping to make realizable the visual richness of this book.

❊ ❊ ❊

Elena Filipovic is director and curator of Kunsthalle Basel. She was senior curator at WIELS, Brussels from 2009–14 and co-curated the 5th Berlin Biennial in 2008 with Adam Szymczyk. She has curated numerous solo exhibitions with emerging artists, in addition to organizing travelling retrospectives of artists from Marcel Duchamp to Alina Szapocznikow, Mark Leckey and Anne Teresa De Keersmaeker. Most recently, she edited *The Artist as Curator: An Anthology* (Mousse Publishing, 2017) and *Felix Gonzalez-Torres: Specific Objects Without Specific Form* (König Books, 2016). She is author of *The Apparently Marginal Activities of Marcel Duchamp* (The MIT Press, 2016).

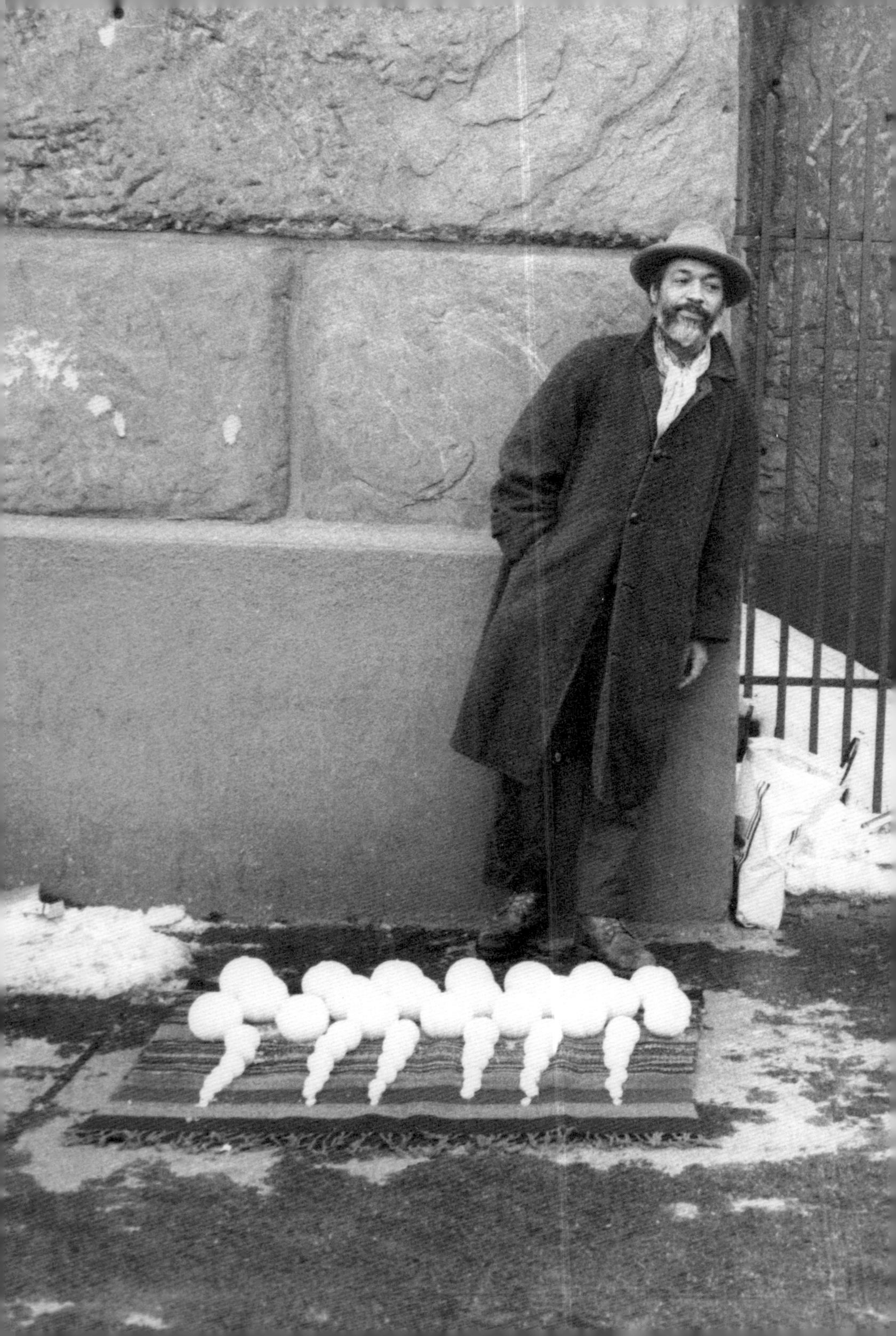

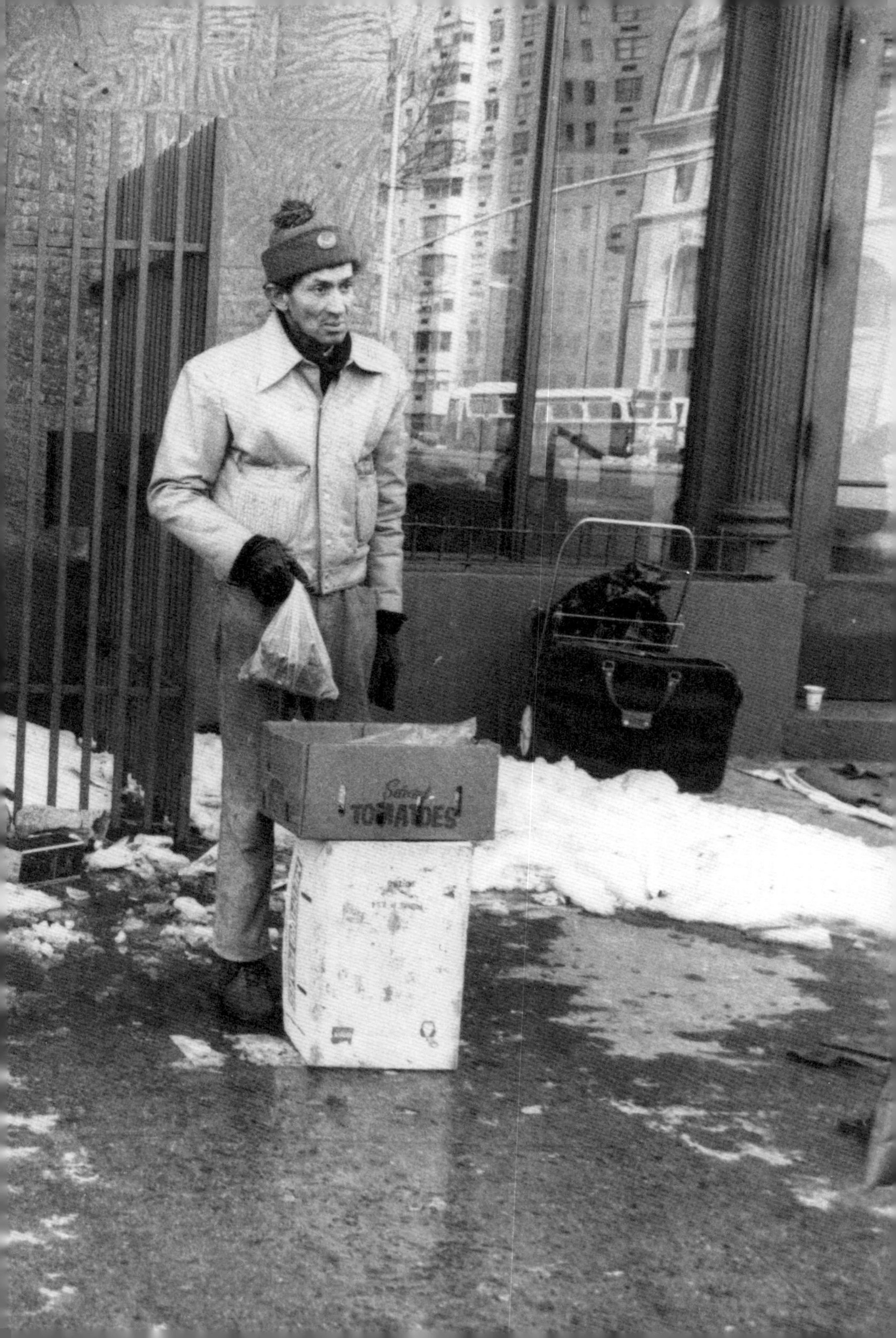
TOMATOES

cover and previous pages:

David Hammons,
Bliz-aard Ball Sale, 1983,
Cooper Square, New York
Photographs: Dawoud Bey
Cover courtesy Tilton Gallery, New York
Previous pages courtesy Exit Art Archives,
Fales Library and Special Collections,
New York University

Contents

Part 1
What We Know

I decided a long time ago that the less I do, the more an artist I am.
– David Hammons[1]

The Images

David Hammons stands poised, a snowball in hand, his face deadpan; rows of carefully organized snowballs are laid out before him on a rug. A portrait of the artist as coolly composed salesman: that is how this photograph reads. There are others: the artist as amused prankster or dapper street peddler as a passer-by laughs at his commodity display; with a child being pushed in a stroller, to whom he offers a free sample, one of the tiniest of his snowballs; with a woman who crouches and poses for a picture while Hammons goofs off in the background; with a man who points at the setup, incredulously; with a young couple as they carefully deliberate his offerings; with a small crowd that has gathered to marvel at and ask about what he is selling. In one image, the artist's outstretched hand meets a buyer's, as if the photographer was trying to capture the exact moment of monetary exchange – a 'money shot' of sorts. In another, an elderly woman stares as Hammons straightens the regimented order of his merchandise; the photographer Dawoud Bey's image catches the bric-a-brac setups of other street sellers in the background. You can almost feel the thickness of the air and lull of time in yet another image as a nearby trader fingers the jewellery he is displaying while Hammons grips his brown-bagged drink and turns to his neighbours. Some pictures are evidently staged portraits, in which the artist's measured calm amidst a bustling scene is striking. Others capture impromptu public reactions and Hammons laughing at it all. A still life of the snowballs shows them forlorn on their rug, without a vendor in sight; also caught in the frame of the photograph are trash, melting snow and secondhand items for sale nearby. Most of these pictures have rarely been seen, and some have never been published at all. Although only a select few images have circulated over the years, dozens more contribute to what little concrete evidence there is of the ephemeral artwork they picture.

The artwork in question is *Bliz-aard Ball Sale*, Hammons's 1983 sale of snowballs on a snowy New York street corner (fig.1–21). Of all the artist's actions, it is undoubtedly the most iconic. Frequently cited and rabidly influential, it is so despite being long known only through the artist's sporadic mentions and a handful of circulated photographs, and despite the fact that very likely the sale itself was not seen by most of the artists, writers, collectors and curators interested in his practice (including this one). Its details remain vague, furtive. We know, or think we know, that Hammons hawked a series of varyingly sized, perfectly formed snowballs amid other street vendors at Cooper Square in New York's East Village. That much we can see from the photographs that were snapped by Bey during the 'event' (although using that word seems wrong, and 'performance' perhaps equally so). No invitation or press release or formal announcement was sent out. It wasn't meant for the art world. And perhaps it did not take place for an 'audience' at all.[2]

The sale was probably held on Sunday 13 February, the day after a massive blizzard hit New York. But even of that seemingly straightforward detail I am not sure.[3] Hammons stood in the cold on the south-east corner of Cooper Square and Astor Place, at the foot of Cooper Union, positioned among the unemployed, the homeless and the generally down-on-their-luck selling the likes of used books, clothing and cassette tapes. The artist presented his differently sized snowballs in neat, graduated rows on a colourful, folded North African rug, answering the questions of whoever approached. The whole of his sale may have lasted about thirty minutes. Or three hours. Or he may have set up in the morning and lasted until nightfall. Or he might have held the sale over multiple days. The story varies, depending on who does the telling.[4]

Similarly, descriptions diverge regarding the process of making and selling the snowballs. One version goes that Hammons made them beforehand and froze them overnight – rendering the balls perfectly compact and hardened – in advance of transporting them to the bustling corner in a shopping cart.[5] Another posits that they were 'one of the more labour-intensive pieces' Hammons had made by that point, as evidenced in their geometric precision and graduated manufacture.[6] But the artist tells it another way, describing their fabrication as easy and made with snow on the spot.[7] They were then sold off individually, each priced at one dollar, as the artist himself insists.[8] Or they were priced according to size, ranging from ten cents to ten dollars, as several witnesses recall.[9] Then again, maybe their price was entirely negotiable, as still another remembers.[10] The 'facts' are fuzzy.

I'm not sure if we will ever know for certain. We do know, however, that the snowballs garnered considerable attention from unknown passers-by who, curious, stopped to look and inquire. Some even carefully contemplated which snowball to purchase, if purchase they did. Others laughed off the whole thing as a ridiculous prank. By the end – or at least so goes Hammons's and indeed most versions of the story – he easily sold just about all of them, raking in a total of about twenty dollars.[11] This, like all anecdotes about the affair, lives on the edge of truth. Among the anecdotes is one that might actually be true, even if it sounds most improbable: at least one snowball, of the larger variety, was either deliberately saved or by chance unsold and, in any case, taken home by Hammons. Like a token, it was preserved in the corner of a borrowed freezer. For years.

But who could hold on to a snowball? Fugitive by nature, the sale's 'objects' were not made to last, even if its myth *was*. No press reported on *Bliz-aard Ball Sale* when it took place. It would take a few years before the first scattered acknowledgements even appeared. Although now considered a lodestar by many, its history has been curiously little pressed. Interviewers, then and since, seem barely to have asked about it. The artist himself has not volunteered much about what happened. Among those that claim to have seen it (their witnessing itself unverifiable), there are glitches of memory and mutually incommensurable accounts. The photos that record the piece show the artist's interaction with potential customers, even their giddy attention, but no image captures a client actually taking a snowball away. Indeed, despite the artist's insistence that he easily sold them off, not a single image shows the display of commodities significantly diminished. So how does one corroborate any of *Bliz-aard Ball Sale*'s stories when memory has faded, or is deliberately withheld? Or when evidence is sparse, and the artwork itself cannot be summoned? The impossibility of verification enshrouds *Bliz-aard Ball Sale* to the point of becoming indistinguishable from it.

The Myth

I would like to be a myth, be on the invisible side of things. The shadow. When you are always seen people get used to that and you aren't a mystery anymore. I've seen it happen many times.
– David Hammons[12]

Everything sacred, that intends to remain so, must cover itself in mystery.
– Léopold Sédar Senghor[13]

Some of what you will read here might, then, be apocryphal. Let's start there. Rarely does history writing want to admit the tentativeness, conjecture, even speculative fabulation at its heart. Yet anything written on David Hammons must, perforce, begin with an admission of doubt. Because Hammons, an artist best known to the art world for his refusal to participate in its rites and rules, has made a life work of tactical evasion. Rumours, myth and hearsay about him abound – often, naturally, contradictory. Perhaps fittingly so, since some of his most significant works – *Bliz-aard Ball Sale* prime among them – have been unabashedly ephemeral, evanescent and unannounced. How, then, could one possibly speak of his work conclusively or factually?

'You'll never get the whole story', says one of his friends, the curator Horace Brockington. He adds, 'The fact that you can't get to David is part of David.'[14] 'He's into the shadows' is the way long-time friend A.C. Hudgins puts it.[15] Meanwhile, Dawoud Bey notes that the artist 'is committed to creating works of art that exist in their own right; in their own time and space. Some of us may never see them. In fact, most of us won't. Yet the sense of myth created by the unseen is one of Hammons's concerns. Not that he preoccupies himself with it. But he understands the implications.'[16]

As if turning on its head Ralph Ellison's haunting line 'I am invisible, understand, simply because people refuse to see me', Hammons made himself difficult to find precisely when the art world went looking for him.[17] His crisp elucidation of his own logic is as follows: 'to be invisible is more powerful than being visible'.[18] Because Hammons knows that to be black in an art world as white as the walls of its museums, and in an America where privilege and presence and whiteness go hand in hand, is to realize that visibility is something to mess with, to disavow. As a result, he rarely accepts requests for interviews, largely dodges the inquiries of scholars, refuses to send out press releases or make artist's statements. He doesn't have a website and isn't officially represented by a gallery. He scorns the art market even as he astutely plays it, selling his work out of his studio, cutting out the middleman; if he does use one, he rigs the conditions of the transaction in his own favour (90% for him, 10% for the gallery, or so it is said). He snubs most invitations to exhibit, and has eschewed retrospective

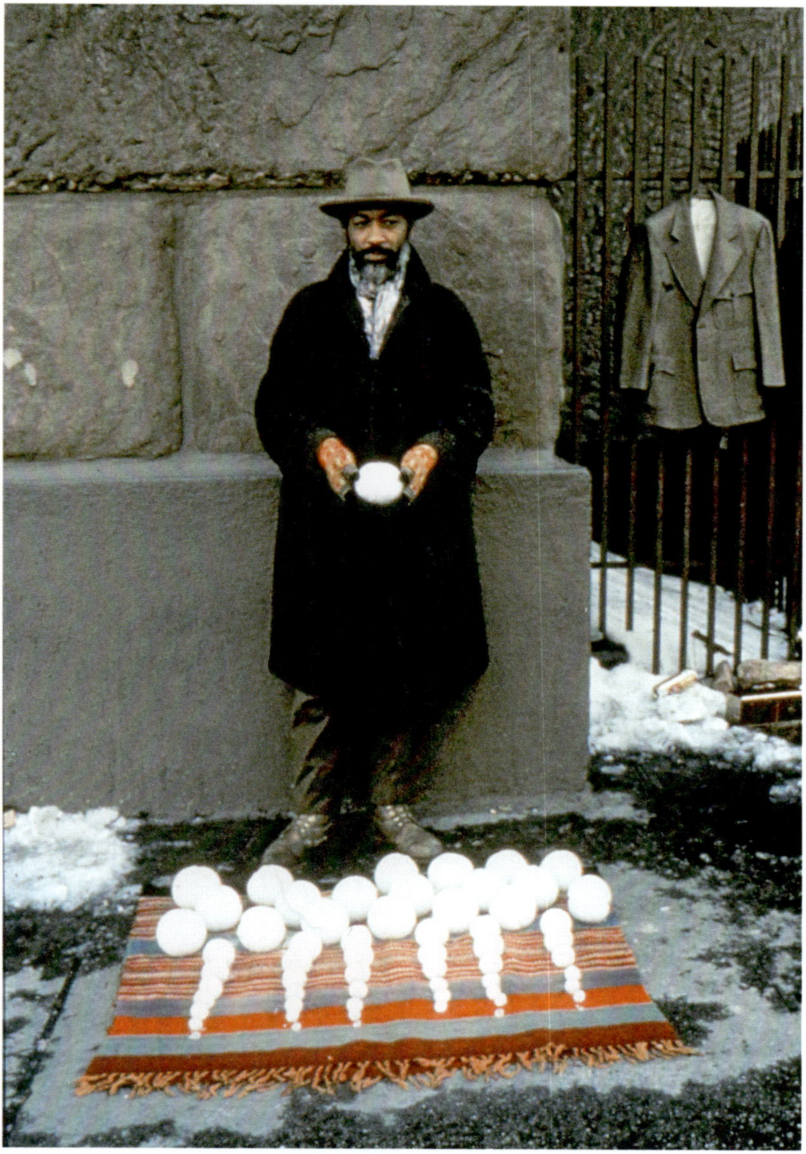

1-19, 21. David Hammons,
Bliz-aard Ball Sale, 1983,
Cooper Square, New York
Photographs: Dawoud Bey
1-10, 15-21. Courtesy Tilton Gallery, New York; 12-14. Courtesy Exit Art Archives, Fales Library and Special Collections, New York University; 11. MoMA P.S.1 Archives, II.A.794, Museum of Modern Art, New York. Digital image © 2022, The Museum of Modern Art, New York/Scala, Florence

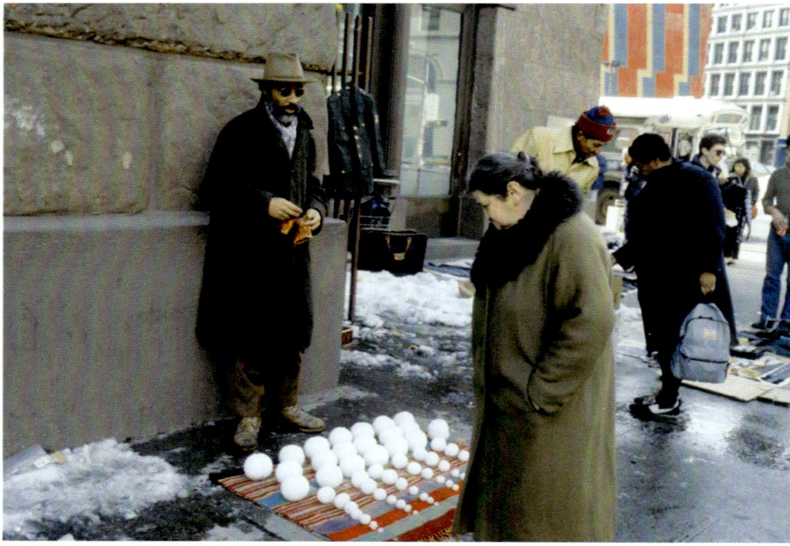

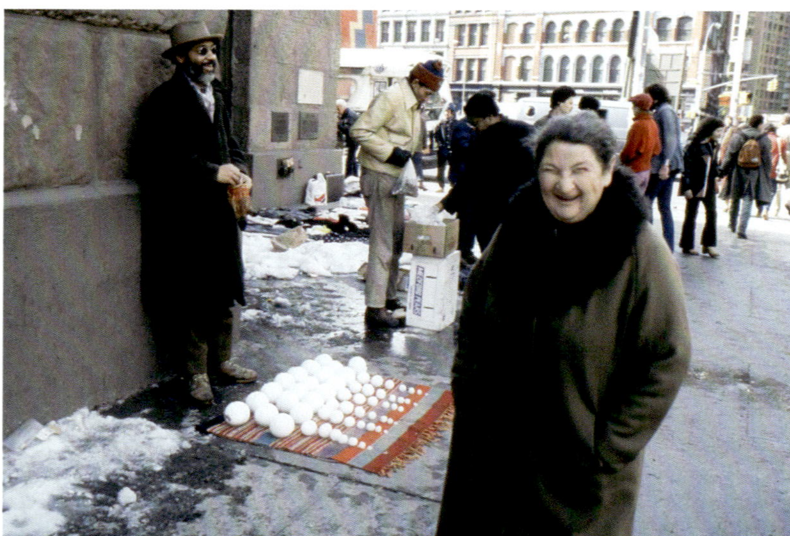

2-3.

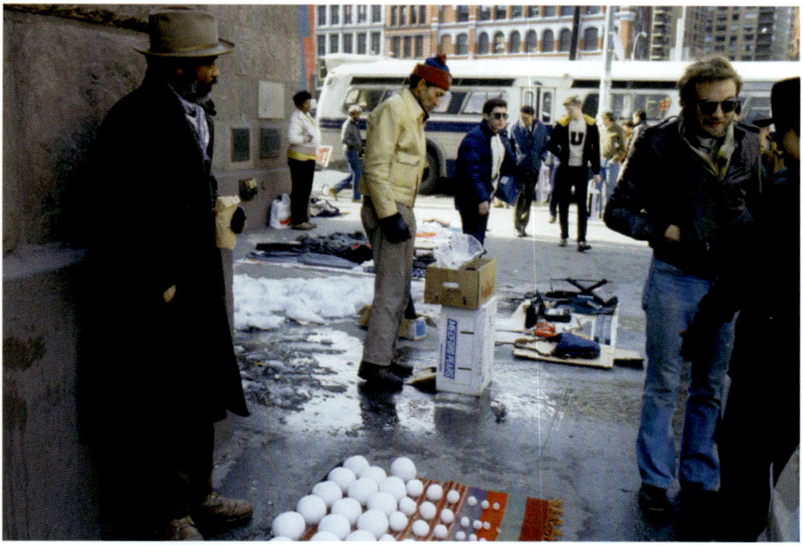

4.

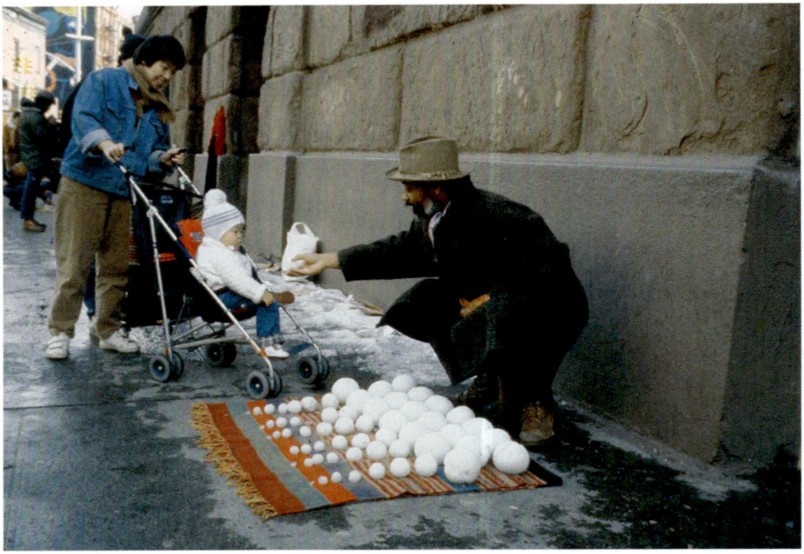

5.

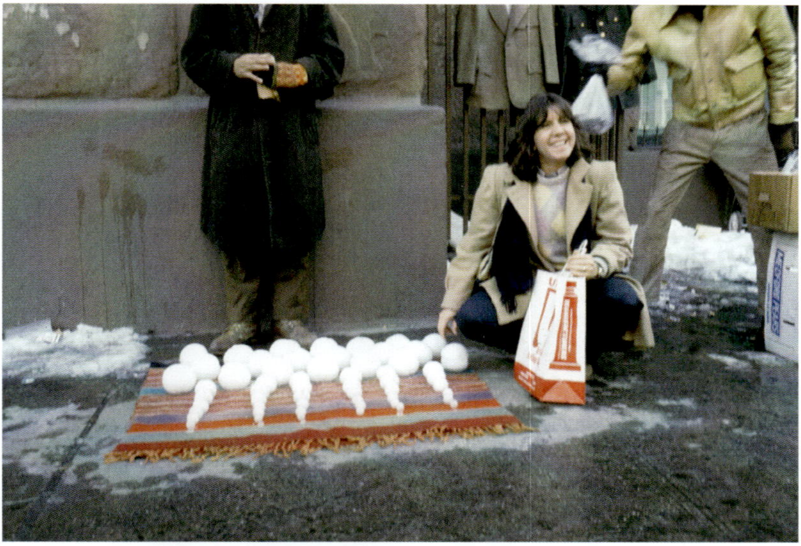

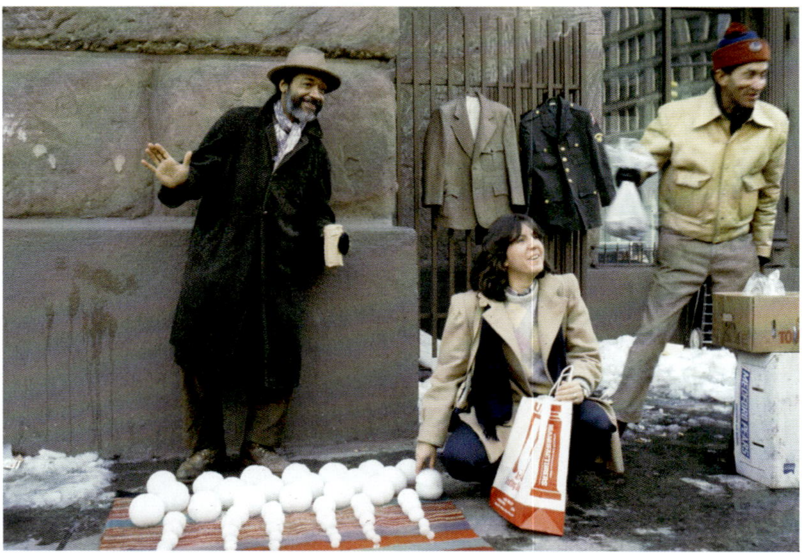

6-7.

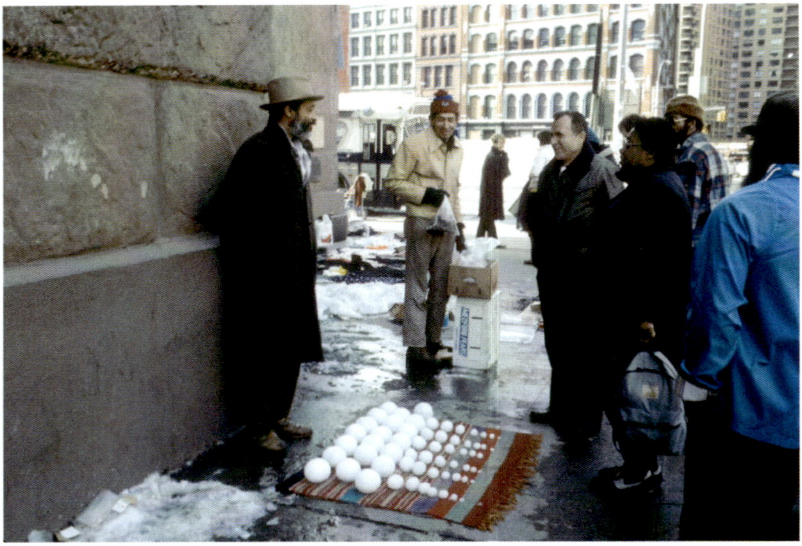

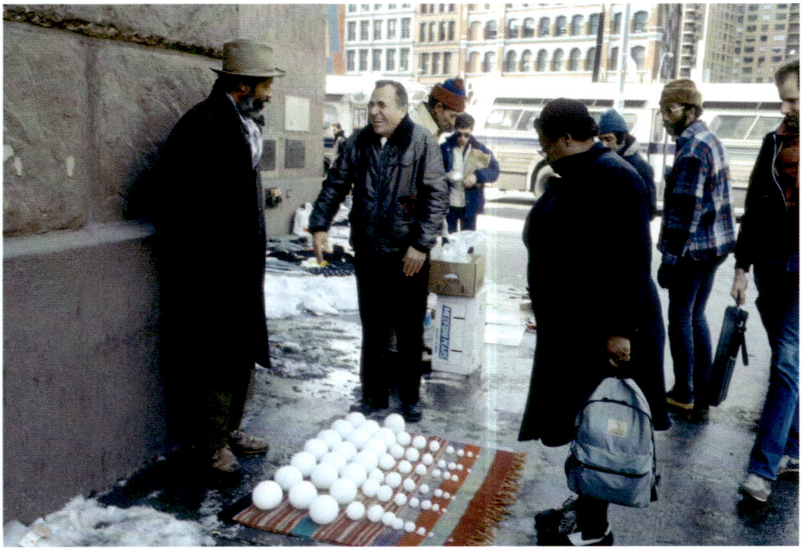

8-9.

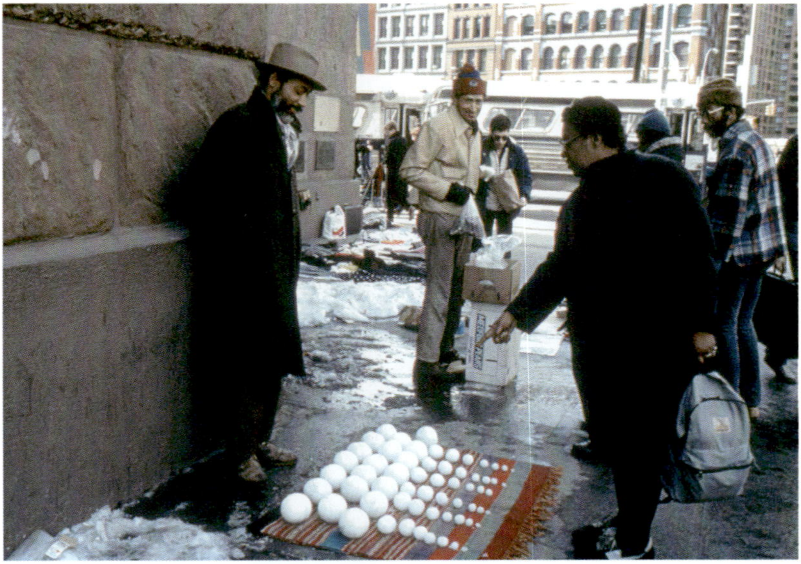

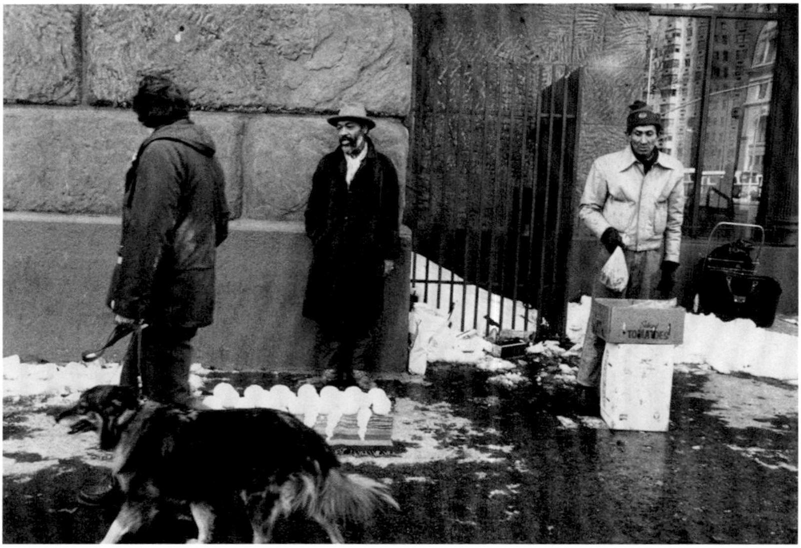

11.

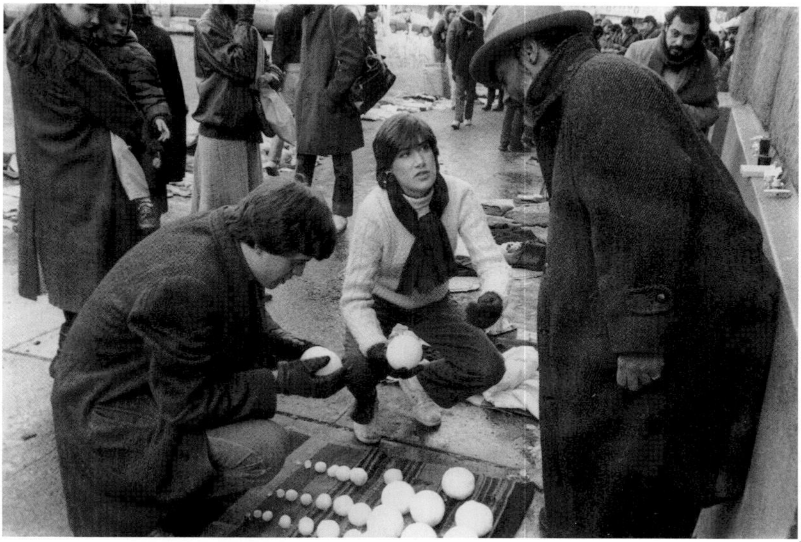

12.

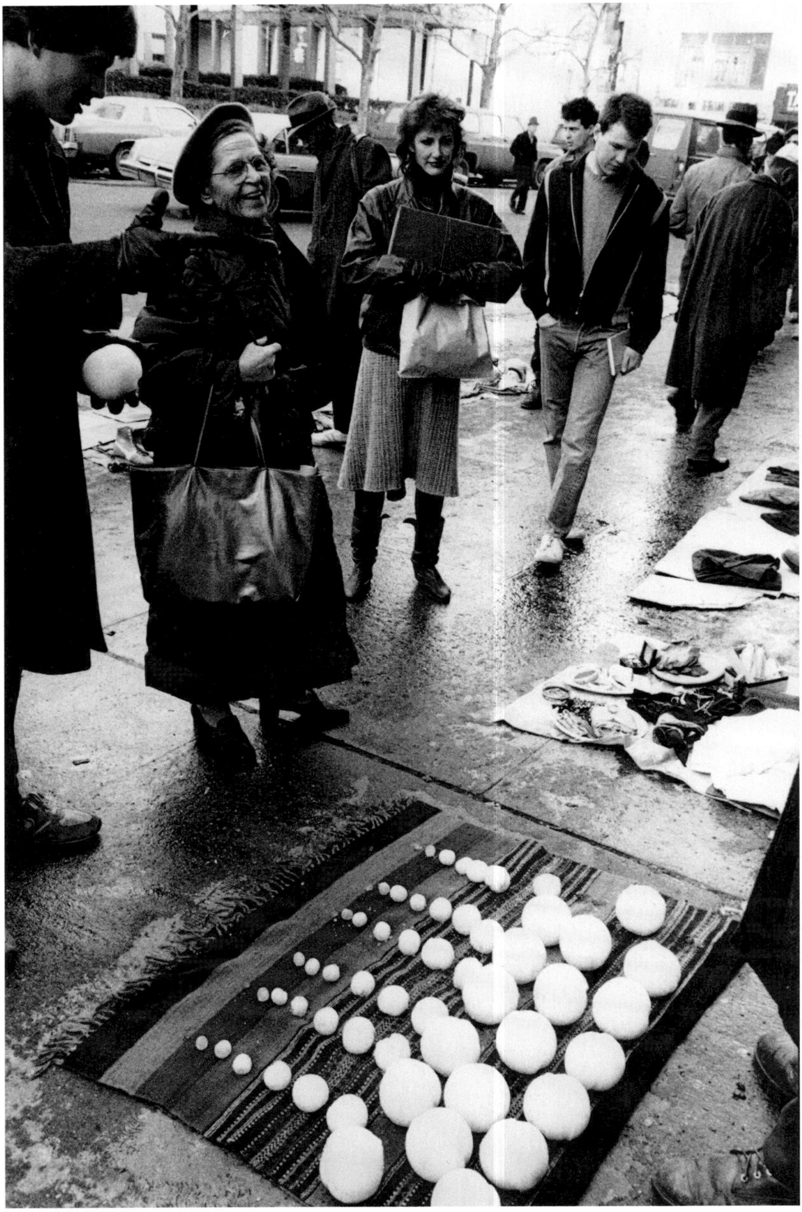

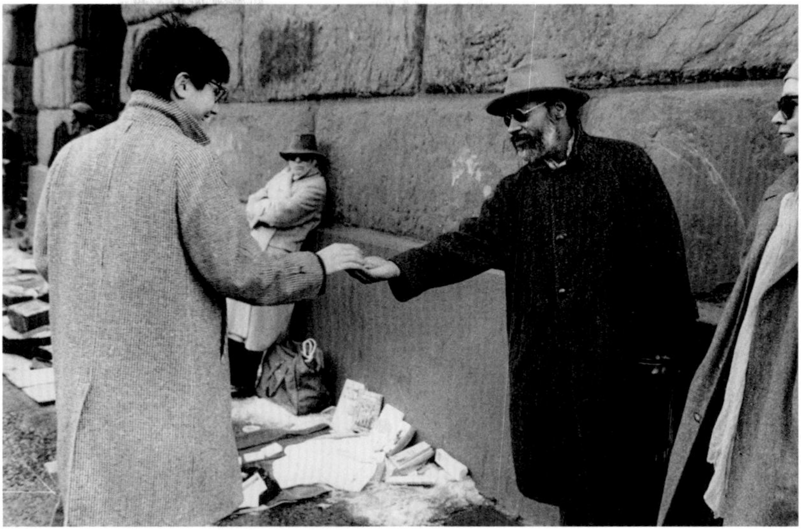

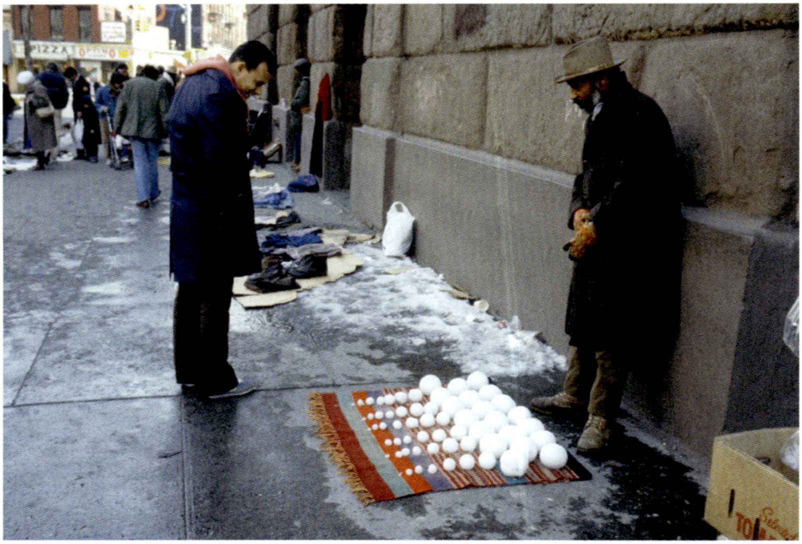

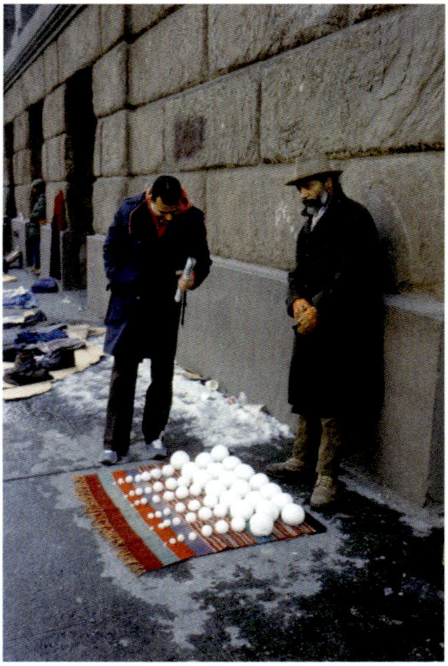

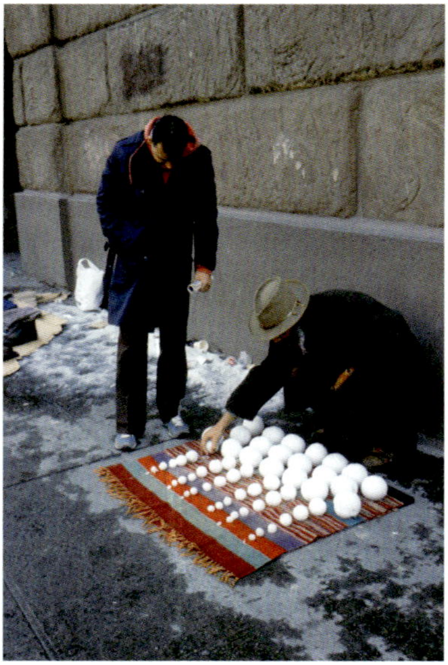

15-17.

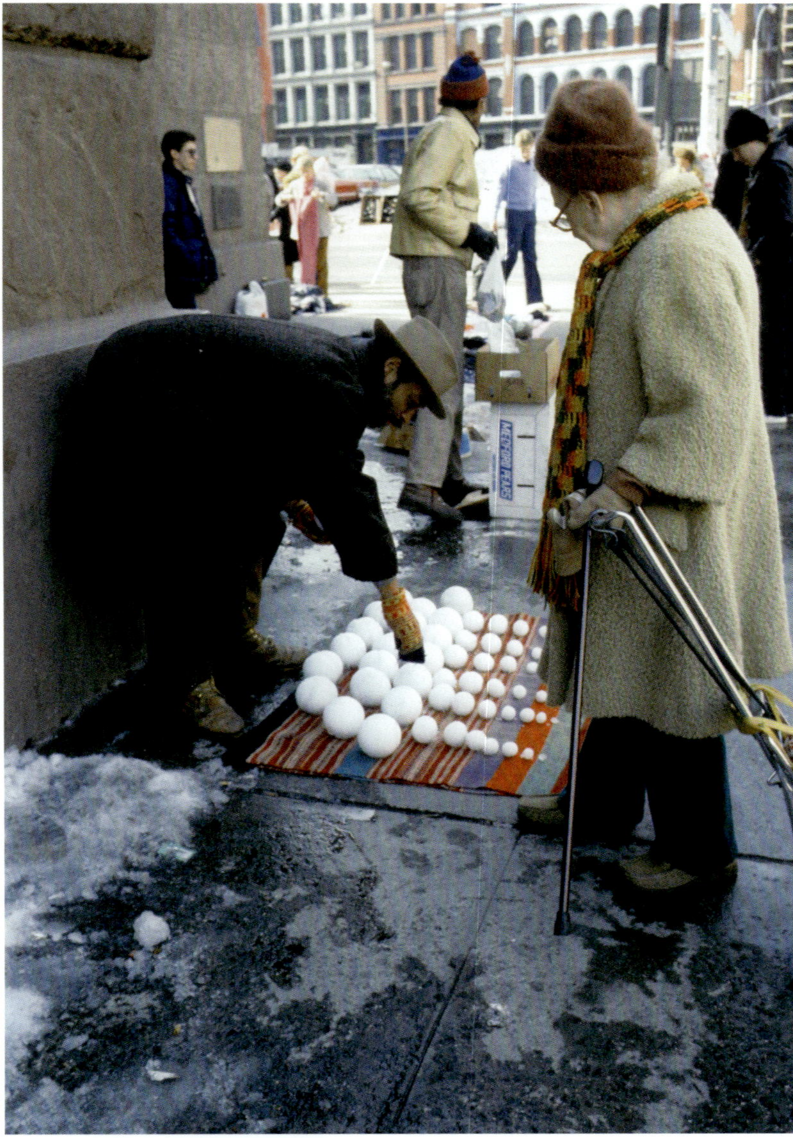

18.

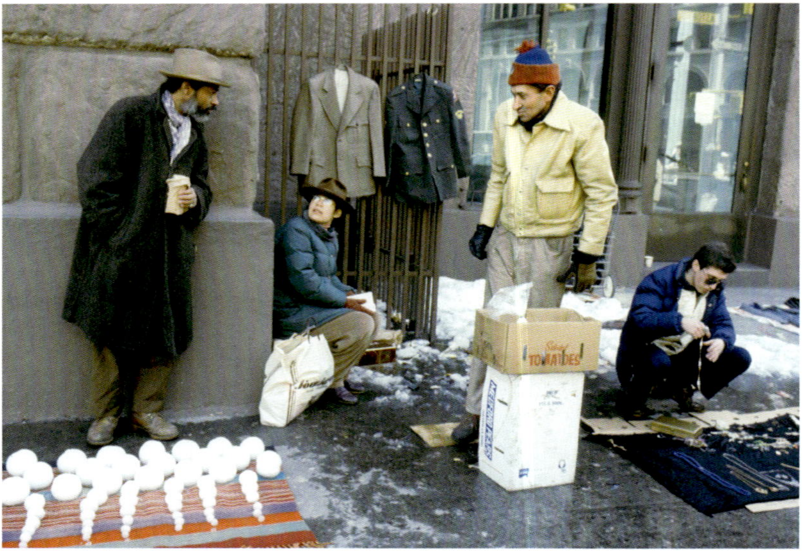

19.

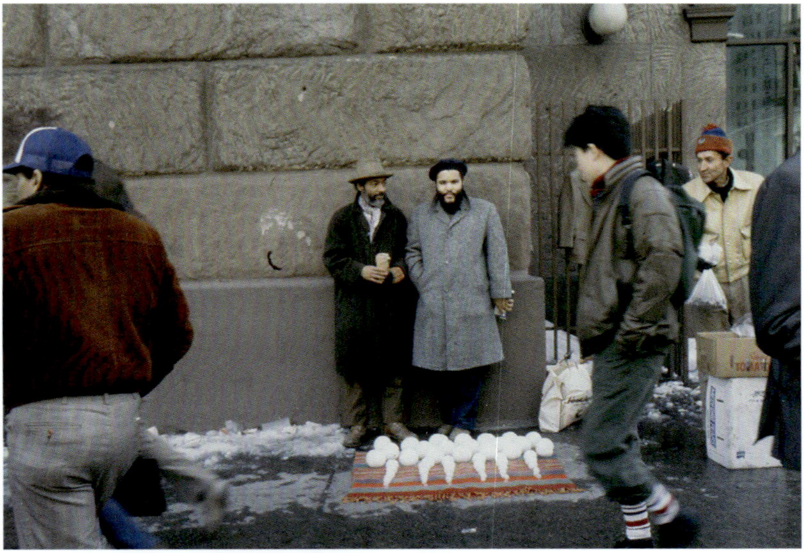

20. David Hammons,
Bliz-aard Ball Sale, 1983,
Cooper Square in New York
(Dawoud Bey poses to the
right of the artist)
Photograph: Candida Alvarez

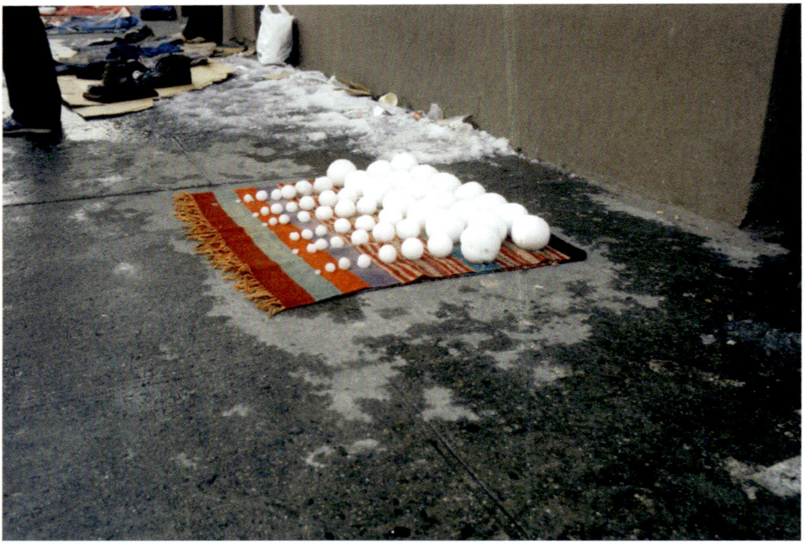

21.

surveys at any number of venerable institutions interested in showing his work. Once he even went so far as to get a lawyer involved to make sure a certain prestigious museum *wouldn't* organize a retrospective devoted to him.[19] He declines, quite simply, to cooperate in the dissemination and promotion – the making widely visible – of an artistic 'oeuvre' of the type that artists are typically preoccupied with.

Rather than trivial anecdotes of one artist's cagey behaviour, all of these accounts describe gestures that occupy the very core of Hammons's larger practice. Arguably, these gestures *are* his practice. That practice is based not on the habitual art-world hope (and hype) for ultimate visibility and omnipresence, but the opposite: wilful obfuscation at the risk of obscurity. As a result, evasiveness – as an operational strategy as much as a form of ethics – hangs over his work like dust in the air. To understand Hammons, then, one must not only note this, as so many articles do, but *pay attention to it.*

To do so is to attempt to meet Hammons's practice on its own terms, which doesn't mean miming its radical stance or pretending to speak in its 'voice', but instead developing a methodology that finds its cues in the operations of the work itself. For if evasion is taken to be an artistic practice (even a medium) with Hammons, it is possible to recognize that his work has all along provoked and problematized the single-minded narration of the incontrovertible facts that are presented as History. And perhaps more forcefully than any of his works, *Bliz-aard Ball Sale* encapsulates the manifold contradictions of this fraught relationship to historical certainty. 'There's a metaphor in ice', Hammons once stated. 'Ice always changes. The process is beautiful. You look at this ice, come back – it's changed its shape.'[20] What if the reading of an artwork could do the same: be shape-shifting and accepting of the impossibility of attaching any singular truth to it?

Bliz-aard Ball Sale's cold, hard facts are fittingly difficult to establish. Maybe, ultimately, those facts are not important at all. The pursuit of the artwork here is thus not about pinning down 'empirical' evidence or establishing anything like the 'truth' behind the myth. And it is even less to ossify it into a monument. Any such attempt would, in any case, betray a project whose radicality is its blatant bid for ephemerality. Instead, to attempt to take *Bliz-aard Ball Sale* seriously is to admit that it was conceived *precisely* to slip between our fingers – to trouble the grasp of the market, as much as of history and knowability.

Part 2
The Evasions of David Hammons

Where He's From

... to become a Negro Man, let alone a Negro artist, one had to make oneself up as one went along. This had to be done in the not-at-all-metaphorical teeth of the world's determination to destroy you. The world had prepared no place for you, and if the world had its way, no place would ever exist.
- James Baldwin[21]

I like being from nowhere; it's a beautiful place. That means I can look at anyone who's from somewhere and see how really caught they are.
- David Hammons[22]

It might seem preposterous to propose that in order to do justice to an action like *Bliz-aard Ball Sale*, which probably lasted just a few hours, you need to look closely at the life trajectory and development of its author. But it would not be so far-fetched to imagine that, just as a snowball picks up layers of snow that cling to its surface as it rolls, Hammons's action was laced with traces of where he is from ('nowhere', he'd tell you) and his studies (however informal or inconsistently documented). It was spiked with attitudes and approaches he had acquired over decades: his keen observation of American urban culture, his attachment to the everyday, his making art from 'readymade' things (often found in street-side dustbins), his relationship to the art world (stand-offish, critical), his complex understanding of and response to race and the language used to speak of it, his construction of a persona and an oeuvre of resistance, and still other 'techniques' that, in retrospect, were nothing less than pivotal. Most important among these practices, however, is how Hammons consistently eludes us, even as we might try to pin him down. Because in this already the artist set a stage for *Bliz-aard Ball Sale*. And that stage is founded on evasion.

Inconsistent biographical details riddle publications on Hammons.[23] Likely this wouldn't happen if the artist kept and distributed a curriculum vitae, or if a designated gallery did so on his behalf. Early on, Hammons elected to dispense with both. He forced institutions interested in his work to draw up their own approximations of his CV based on what they could find (the inevitable circulation of misinformation resulted). He once even insisted on publishing the handwritten index cards produced by a friend's child on the occasion of an elementary school 'show-and-tell' presentation on him; they appeared in a 1992 exhibition catalogue, in place of his résumé or an essay about his work.[24] You get the sense that he prefers silence over declaration, rumour over fact, the impermanent over the durable, oral histories over written; and that he prefers, indeed, that the narrations of his life and work might be enveloped in a fog of caveats, contradiction and, ultimately, doubt.

Fittingly, and probably not true to the last detail, this account of his background perhaps comes as close to actuality as any other: Born David Raymond Hammons on 24 July 1943 in Springfield, Illinois, he was the youngest of ten children. While he was growing up, his father was almost entirely absent, except for impromptu appearances 'maybe twice a year' as the son remembers.[25] During one passage through town, his father sat on a bus across from the young Hammons, who quietly watched him without his father realizing it – so little was Hammons Sr involved with his children. And, perhaps most tellingly, so ready was the youngest Hammons to remain invisible, already then, when he was not recognized where he should have been.[26] His mother supported the family with various odd jobs, although, the artist admits, to this day he has no idea how they got by. Ten children crammed into a tiny house one block from the railroad in precarious conditions, with three to a bed, hand-me-down clothes and the air wailing with the sound of trains: these conditions defined Hammons's beginnings. But so, too, did the fact that perhaps because everyone else in his family was older and busy scrambling to make ends meet, he was, as he says, 'left to grow up in my own fantasy'.[27]

The summer Hammons was born, race riots broke out in Mobile, Alabama; Beaumont, Texas; Detroit; and in Harlem, New York City. His hometown of Springfield, itself a midsized Midwestern town and the capital of Illinois, abided a 'Southern-style' bigotry. It was a time when Confederate flags still hung proudly and profligately in windows, when African Americans could only sit in the balcony seats of the local Orpheum Theater, when different nights were designated for blacks and whites at the local ice skating rink, and the public pools were decisively off limits to blacks. As a result, Hammons admits to never having learned to swim, instead trying his hand at basketball, one of the few sports open to black youth and easy to play quite simply because it was the cheapest game around. He went on to practice anywhere between six and seven hours a day, by his own account.[28] But when he stopped growing, having reached five feet eight inches, his hopes of a career in the sport were thwarted, and he put his skin in another game.

Hammons wasn't what you would call a devoted student. He made one of his more telling and oft-cited statements when he insistently told Kellie Jones in 1986: 'I've never, ever liked art, ever.'[29] The fact is, the art he was exposed to in school didn't make the field seem very welcoming – it was a pantheon of whiteness, through and through. His exposure to cultural forms not officially called art came through Claude Champ, a foster-grandfather of sorts, the man whose wife had raised Hammons's mother. Champ tricked out his home and front yard with everyday objects whose spiritual charge connected them back to ancient Kongo and Angolan traditions. The first to probe Hammons regarding his exposure to these traditions was Robert Farris Thompson, the eminent Yale historian of African culture, whose 1983 book *Flash of the Spirit: African and Afro-American Art and Philosophy* was a touchstone for the many African-American artists who regularly went to hear him lecture in the 1980s and 90s.[30] Hammons recalled to Thompson that Champ whitewashed the trees and telephone poles outside his house, and the stones that marked the boundaries of his property, and encircled flower beds in heart forms (for the attraction of affection) or star forms (references to heaven); following ancient traditions, Thompson observed, Champ was creating 'mystic barriers' and turning his yard into an '*nkisi*, a spatial charm'.[31] The distinctly African symbology of this homespun magic incited the young Hammons's imagination, even acting, as Thompson suggests, as 'a secret education, beyond the West, shaping and grounding his sensibility'.

In June 1963, when he was twenty, and just a few years after Champ died, Hammons left Illinois for California, to live with an older sister in Los Angeles. There he held his share of odd jobs, from church janitor to assistant in a frame shop. He even accepted at least one commission, from a cheap hotel requesting polite flower paintings appropriate for guest rooms and hallways. He did not consider this his art, and he cannily signed the paintings with a pseudonym, later disavowing them.[32] Liberal arts schools kicked him out, telling him that he would be better off in trade school. He began to pursue the commercial arts, enrolling at Los Angeles City College for a year, transferring to advertising arts at the Los Angeles Trade Technical College for another, dropping out and moving on to study fine art at the Chouinard Art Institute (which later became California Institute of the Arts, or CalArts) from 1966–68. And from 1968–72, he took night and weekend classes at Otis Art Institute.

The above itinerary of studies has speckled biographies of Hammons, despite the fact that official records of his presence are not always entirely consistent with these accounts. Too poor to afford to register for each and every semester, or perhaps understanding that formal enlistment in an institutional structure wasn't always an utter necessity, a young Hammons may occasionally have 'enrolled' by simply hanging out in school cafeterias and hallways to be close to art students, to absorb what they were learning.[33] He has recounted that he started experimenting with body prints after seeing students trying out the method in a Chouinard classroom that he looked into as he was walking down the hall.[34] Shortly after, at Otis, he encountered the professor and master printer-draftsman Charles White, whose attitude and model as a black artist would have a lasting influence on Hammons.[35] His early years studying advertising art surely had an impact too. We know he abandoned the field because working for clients and having deadlines was anathema to his way of being.[36] But it could also be surmised that, like Andy Warhol before him, the logic of advertising had taught Hammons how scarcity/elusiveness might fan the flame of consumer desire. (In Warhol's case, it was an overexposure that kept the self in absentia.)

Married by 1966, he was living with his wife in her parents' house in the Los Angeles neighbourhood of Crenshaw, making art in the garage and selling the results from the trunk of his car.[37] This art included, at the beginning, enamel paintings on Masonite. These rather conventional abstract explosions of colour might not have taken him far, but Hammons would soon enough forge a new aesthetic vocabulary for himself, fostered at least in part by his coming of age as an artist in an LA that had given rise to Simon Rodia's eccentric architectural agglomeration of scrap known as the Watts Towers, built during the 1920s–50s; an LA that had opened Marcel Duchamp's first retrospective in 1963; an LA that nourished the budding avant-garde performance art of the likes of Chris Burden and

Senga Nengudi; an LA that became a stronghold of the Black Arts Movement; an LA that was suddenly set aflame in 1965, at the time of the 'Watts riots'. Though the Civil Rights Act had been signed into federal law in 1964, and California would ratify the Equal Rights Amendment in 1972, both during Hammons's early Los Angeles years, the country as a whole seemed not quite ready to contend with the ideas of race upon which its empire had been built. In 1963, the year Hammons arrived in LA, four young black girls were killed by white supremacists in a church bombing in Birmingham, Alabama. In 1964, the bodies of three civil rights volunteers working to register black voters in Mississippi were found murdered by the Klu Klux Klan. 1964 was also the same year that Martin Luther King Jr won the Nobel Peace Prize, only to be shot dead in Memphis four years later. In 1965, the African-American teenagers known as the Harlem Six were tried for crimes they didn't commit – in an era before dashboard cameras and citizens' digital recordings, police brutality of blacks was not only rampant and unpunished, but undocumented, unacknowledged and unpublicized. All of this served as the backdrop to the 1966 birth of the Black Panther Party. This, too, was the backdrop of Hammons's practice.[38]

Making a Stereotype Literal

In the late 1960s, Hammons made his studio in a large former dance hall on Slauson Avenue in LA. There he developed his first body prints, which inescapably referenced Yves Klein's early 1960s *Anthropométries*. Spectacularly, Klein's works were made at staged, black-tie events, where the artist himself appeared in a tuxedo and a chamber orchestra performed a concert of classical music as naked, voluptuous women drenched in the French artist's signature International Klein Blue pressed their bodies onto blank canvases and swathes of paper, surfaces that would become framed 'paintings'. These were events for the bourgeoisie, with all the refined trappings of patriarchal European culture. Hammons borrowed the technique, left out the event and refigured the content: his retorts were made with margarine, slicked onto his own body to thus imprint blank sheets of paper; he then dusted the resulting forms with dark, sifted pigment made from powdered chalk, which easily clung to the grease. The artist swapped Klein's invariably white nudes for his own racialized body, declaring, 'I was using a Klein technique to achieve a Charles White feel.'[39]

Photographs of the artist in his studio show him shirtless and prone, pressing and smearing himself against large expanses of paper (fig.26). He sought out a one-to-one imprint of his body onto the page, and he sometimes printed it to appear draped in an American flag, or toting a paper bag containing a bottle of wine (fig.23, 24). Explicitly haunting the beginnings of his body prints, he acknowledges, is the 'moral obligation' he felt 'as a black artist to try to graphically document what I feel socially'.[40] Some prints incorporated allusions to black unrest in the 1960s and early 70s: a judge's order that Bobby Seale, co-founder of the Black Panthers, be bound and gagged during the Chicago Eight trial in 1969; black students' painful struggle to be admitted to the University of Mississippi (leading to deaths, rioting and the intervention of the National Guard); or the tragedy of black men turning to alcohol to dull the effects of poverty and humiliation.[41]

Racial tumult inheres in these works, like pigment in margarine. Similar to the relation between a fingerprint and the digit that made it, or a weathervane and the wind that pushed it, Hammons's chosen method was an attempt to retain a palpable - indexical - grip on the real.[42] As the artist notes in a rare, early filmed interview, he had turned to body prints instead of painting because he needed to embody a 'truth', suggesting that the very nature of the indexical print would somehow *stand in* for him (and even for 'us', as he says to the black film-maker Ulysses Jenkins recording him).[43] As with so much of Hammons's subsequent work, these pieces juxtapose seemingly conflicting messages, as in *Spade (Power to the Spade)*, from 1969, where the raised fist of Black Power and the prominent lips of racist caricature are held in an unresolved contradiction with a symbolic slur (fig.25). Instead of a picture of heroic uplift and dignified celebration (or its opposite: oppression, victimization), blackness here is not an unequivocal condition, but instead the product of contradictory forces. That is the image's 'truth'.

It was on a visit to New York in 1970 that Hammons encountered the work of Melvin Edwards, whose sculptures and installations made with chains and barbed wire spoke to the African-American condition through a form of materially loaded abstraction. It was a revelation, Hammons has admitted - the first abstract art he had seen 'that had cultural value in it for black people'.[44] The encounter prompted him to forge his own object production that could also evoke blackness through material assemblage rather than pictorial representation. Just a few years later, in 1972, on a visit to the Field Museum of Natural History in Chicago, he and fellow artist Betye Saar marvelled at a ceremonial robe adorned with sewn-on balls of African hair on display in the museum's basement, where the African and Oceanic art was shown. Interpreting the object's celebration of hair as 'a cultural critique of a history of shame', both of the artists were deeply inspired by the object.[45] Hammons's subsequent work involved an even more determined material use of symbols of blackness to evoke painful realities. Sometimes he flaunted these symbols; sometimes he caricatured them, turning their meaning inside out. Because, and of this Hammons was sure, 'outrageously magical things happen when you mess around with a symbol'.[46]

As with the implicit riposte that the body prints advance, Hammons's *Spade* series (made between 1971–74, comprising rusty found digging instruments combined with a saxophone or chains) irreverently tackles racial stereotypes: 'I was trying to figure out why black people were called spades as opposed to clubs. I remember being called a spade once, and I didn't know what it meant; nigger I knew but spade I still don't. So, I just took the shape.'[47] Just as he repeatedly utilized the image of the drunk 'wino' in his body prints, with his *Spade* series Hammons unabashedly took the derogatory cliché as his point of departure. And 'by making a stereotype literal' – a deliberate 'dumbing down', as Manthia Diawara has quoted Hammons saying – the stereotype is twisted, played (like an instrument) and ultimately stripped of its power.[48]

Hammons has also made spade shapes from leather or cardboard, sometimes running over them with his car and spattering them with red paint before photographing them (as with the 1972 *Murder Mystery*, also known as *Spade Run Over by a Volkswagen*), digging them into the earth (his own brand of 'earth work', as he has joked) or hanging them from trees (picture it: that slur for blacks, dangling like 'strange fruit') (fig.27).[49] These were political retorts to his time and to the racialized biases embedded in the mainstream art world, but they also mark the beginnings of his performative practice, in which process is just as important as the thing itself (at times more so). Here, too, began the taste for unconventional presentation locations and strategies that he would return to throughout the rest of his career, and famously in *Bliz-aard Ball Sale*.

On the surface, *Bliz-aard Ball Sale*, made just over a decade later, might seem of another order: it stands as one of the major pieces by Hammons *not* to address race in an explicit way. But to register how the realities of America's racial divide propelled Hammons's early works is to notice how complex and, at times, deliberately provocative was the artist's response to the history of blackness, and to see that race, even when confronted, was not always exactly where you might think it would be. Race, in Hammons's works, could be evasive, too.

Outside

I always admired the renegades, Duchamp and those cats. I've always thought the outside was the place to be.
- David Hammons[50]

Hammons started off exhibiting his art in church basements or on pegboards in Jewish recreation centres since 'they were the only places in Los Angeles that gave shows to black artists'.[51] He was also 'showing around swimming pools ... putting art on trees ... I've been in bars, showing in barbershops and cafés. I've done all that.' In other words, he *made* his own exhibition contexts when more official options were not yet open to him.

It was in the late 1960s and early 70s that he began showing at Suzanne Jackson's short-lived Gallery 32 and at the Brockman Gallery, run by brothers Dale Brockman Davis and Alonzo Davis. Both galleries were artist-run and among the only commercial venues in Los Angeles committed to featuring the work of African-American artists in a highly segregated city.[52] There, alongside the likes of Betye Saar, John Outterbridge, Noah Purifoy and Timothy Washington, Hammons found inspiration and his first commercial-presentation contexts. To look at photographs of Hammons's openings in those years is to see a somewhat different image of the artist than we now know: he wears what looks every bit like a Sunday church suit as he chats with collectors for one Brockman event; he stands at ease next to his art at another opening (a pose, it is said, he shuns today - he has refused to attend his own openings for years) (fig.22, 25). Although he was hardly as evasive then as he would soon become, he was irascible from the start. On this, everyone agrees.

Maybe jazz was responsible. It played an important role for Hammons as a reference in his work and as something to model his own attitude on. To have seen Hammons hawking snowballs in 1983 (or to look now at the images) is to realize that he was the consummate image of 'cool', a cultural attitude theorized by Robert Farris Thompson as a form of black cultural power.[53] Glenn Ligon rightly notes that Hammons 'certainly dressed like a jazz musician: beautiful suits, polished shoes, hats. For example, check out his mohair coat, scarf and multicoloured knitted mittens in the photos of his *Bliz-aard Ball Sale*.'[54] Beyond a vestimentary style, those close to the artist understood Hammons's elusiveness, indeed his very relationship to the art world, as inspired by jazz musicians: '[He] treats the art world with contempt and gets away with it. The more he tells the art world where to go, the more he's in demand. [...] Now, where he learned that is from people like Miles Davis, jazz musicians. The less Miles played in New York, the more money he made. And David's the same way. The less he shows, the more they want him.'[55] For his part, Hammons has often claimed music as the only true black art form – a form to which the visual arts needs to catch up.[56] To 'interpret' his work, he once went so far as to suggest, you shouldn't write about him at all. Instead, 'write about Sun Ra and Miles.'[57] Early works, like *Bird* (1973), from the *Spade* series and dedicated to Charlie Parker, anticipated the central place jazz would have in Hammons's oeuvre, carried through his frequent integration of music into installations and his organization of live concerts as part of his exhibitions over the years, including Sun Ra and his Arkestra playing on the collaborative installation *Delta Spirit* (also known as *Spirit House*) in 1985 (fig.44) and Jameel Moondoc and The Jus Grew Orchestra playing at the 1990 'Rousing the Rubble' opening at P.S.1. Maybe more than any direct reference, however, what we might see in Hammons is that 'near-tragic, near-comic lyricism' that Ralph Ellison associated with the blues, a lyricism born from the desire 'to keep the painful details and episodes of a brutal experience alive in one's aching consciousness, to finger its jagged grain, and to transcend it'.[58]

The Bad Guy

1974, Hammons has said, was a turning point: 'Then I became more abstract and less figurative. Trying to create a hyroglyphics [*sic*] that was definitely black, but ... wasn't in the figurative form.'[59] Hammons started spending more and more time in New York City, which became his primary base shortly after the opening of his show at California State University, Los Angeles in 1974. When he arrived in New York in the mid-1970s, it was a painters' town, as he has recalled, adding, 'If you weren't painting you could forget it. And I was doing body prints.' As it happens, those body prints were meeting with rather easy commercial success by then. *The Wine Leading the Wine* (1969, fig.23) had sold for a cool $1,000, which was reason enough to stop making them: 'I had to get out of the body prints because they were doing so well. I was making money hand-over-fist. But I had run out of ideas... It took me about two years to find something else to do.' His goal became to try to imagine 'an abstract art that wasn't saleable', which led him to fabricate artworks from 'brown paper bags with hair, barbecue bones and grease thrown on them'. After all, who would pay good money for such things? 'Other Black artists here couldn't understand why you would do it if you couldn't sell it.'[60]

It was a time when 'everybody was just grovelling and Tomming – anything to be in the room with some money'. He recalls, 'There were no bad guys here, so I said, "Let me be a bad guy", or attempt to be a bad guy, or play with the bad areas and see what happens.'[61] He did so by making and showing 'outrageous art' that 'no one will buy'.[62] For his first exhibition in New York, in 1975 at Just Above Midtown (affectionately known as JAM, one of the only commercial galleries in the city for contemporary black artists, and run by the intrepid Linda Goode Bryant), he glued African-American hair trimmings that he had collected and shaped into geometric patterns onto grease-smeared paper bags from a local fry joint, adorning some pieces further with dangling, glitter-sprinkled barbecued ribs. Titling the exhibition 'Greasy Bags and Barbecue Bones', Hammons wasn't shy about refusing to make polite, cherishable things, nor about announcing the down-home materials he was using to do so. The result caused a veritable scandal: the black art community attending the opening debated, fiercely, what to make of this 'LA artist' and the image of African Americans he was constructing.[63]

A year later, for a second JAM show, Hammons brought his pieces, including a number of works made from the wire of repurposed coat hangers and African-American hair, on the bus with him from Los Angeles, packed in his bag inside two poster tubes. These were stored in the hallway outside of JAM in the days before Hammons was to begin installing; but so little did it all look like 'art', in fact, that the works were simply thrown away by garbage collectors. Hammons enlisted A.C. Hudgins, part-time assistant at JAM at the time, to troll Harlem's barbershops gathering hair for him to (re)make the works for the show.[64] For *Hair Pyramids* (1976), the artist carefully moulded the barbershop sweepings into a landscape of miniature pyramids arranged along JAM's floor (fig.30). More hair was balled-up and erected as 'wall drawings' - threaded along rubber bands or wire (a pun that put 'Afros' on wires because blacks were described as having 'wiry' hair). Or sometimes hair was braided into elaborate dreadlock tapestries.[65] The charged material appeared in different forms in the various group shows he participated in around the same time, including an exhibition in honour of Martin Luther King Jr at the Los Angeles Municipal Art Gallery, where Hammons showed various works made from greasy paperbags adorned with hair and ribs, including *Lady with Bones* (1976, destroyed and re-made with alterations in 1990) and a sprawling rubberband hair 'drawing' (fig.29). Many of these pieces stunk and left traces of hair grease and fry oil on the museum's or the gallery's walls. No wonder almost no one wanted to buy the works when they were first shown.[66]

In the years that followed, Hammons threaded empty wine bottles into elaborate sculptures (*Untitled*, c.1983, fig.43); nailed thousands of bottle caps and rubber doll shoes to an ephemeral shanty structure he built with Angela Valeria and Jerry Barr from used scraps of wood and other debris (*Delta Spirit*); turned smoked ribs and tyre inner tubes into a wall sculpture (*Wall Piece*, 1989, fig.48); attached deep-fried chicken wings to cheap costume jewellery (*Untitled (Fried Chicken Drumsticks and Chains)*, 1990, fig.49); gave razor-cut hairstyles to stones covered with 'nappy' hair (*Untitled (Rock Head)*, 1990, fig.50); created installations built from moulting hair, teabags, rocks and mud (*Untitled*, 1992, fig.56); and powdered the walls of museums with dirt (notably at the exhibition 'David Hammons: Hometown', Illinois State Museum, 1993, fig.58) - to name just a few examples.[67] Hammons's oeuvre, a mix of handcrafted and found elements, often from the street, is strangely charged: at once modest, wonky and witty, but also inexplicably commanding. The works are witchy things, even when they are so fugitive as to sometimes barely be 'there' at all - as in exhibitions filled with little more than blue light (among them

'Blues and the Abstract Truth', Kunsthalle Bern, 1997, fig.61), 'drawings' made from dust (among them *Untitled (Dust Drawing)*, c.2001, fig.62) or rumours spread as art, each of which Hammons has also made. Or snow packed and sold on a street corner one winter day. To see the photographs, for instance, of how many people stopped in their tracks to look at *Bliz-aard Ball Sale* is to know that despite its utter simplicity, it, too, was inexplicably commanding.

The artists's influences have been, from the start, culturally diverse, ranging from the Tao to the Black Panthers, and from the Kongo *nkisi* tradition to the post-War avant-garde.[68] But few art-historical references have been as recurrent or vital for him as Marcel Duchamp, apparently inciting Hammons's ire and admiration in equal measure.[69] If the father of the readymade is an indelible influence, it was Duchamp's posture as an artist – his ironic detachment from the art world, all while being a consummate player in it – that must have attracted Hammons, too. After all, it was Duchamp who declared that he had 'retired' from art-making already in the 1920s, only to produce a sizeable body of work in the nearly half century that followed; it was Duchamp who, decades later, rented a secret studio to clandestinely work for twenty years on building *Étant donnés: 1° la chute d'eau, 2° le gaz d'eclairage* (*Given: 1. The Waterfall 2. The Illuminating Gas*, 1946–66), his final, elaborate artwork, devised to infiltrate a museum, the better to shake it from within. Breeder of dust, caster of shadows, lover of puns, a man who regularly declared that he was merely a 'breather', and who advocated that artists go 'underground', Duchamp knew how to find beauty in the everyday, and just as importantly, he knew how to be evasive.[70]

Exit

As an artist I'm not aligned with the collectors or the dealers or the museums; I see them all as frauds.
– David Hammons[71]

Marginality and Hammons go hand in hand: marginal materials, marginal venues, marginal visibility. This was the case even before he had the hard-won luxury to turn down institutional invitations and dictate the terms of his sales. Throughout the 1970s, 80s and even into the early 90s, Hammons got by on the occasional sale of artworks (which, after he put an end to the body prints, amounted to selling mostly to a single patron, the same A.C. Hudgins who had helped the artist reconstitute his exhibition at JAM after his artworks were mistakenly thrown away) and with various grant applications that friends helped him write.[72] And though the array of grants he received in the 1980s is impressive, his was a modest and peripatetic existence.[73] He spent years without a bank account, credit card or telephone of his own (something critics commented on throughout the 1990s). Even when he did finally get a phone, he rarely gave out his number or admitted to having one. To find him, you needed to know where to hang out. And then you'd have to wait. Sometimes for a very long time.[74] For over a decade, Hammons slept on random couches or floors, and showered in the homes of friends or girlfriends; through the 90s, his only address was a Harlem studio space without hot water, shower, kitchen or even regular electricity (as attested to by the extension cords one curator saw siphoning off power from the building's hallway) (fig.54).[75] He had grown up in such extreme poverty that perhaps such drifting wasn't much of a nuisance. Or maybe his resistance to living with the sort of amenities so desired by middle-class America was an effort, simply, 'not to lose the spirit'.[76]

Throughout the 80s, Hammons exhibited regularly, even if the mainstream art world hadn't yet taken notice. There were, of course, the countless unannounced street actions, *Bliz-aard Ball Sale* and others, but he was also a fixture, for instance, in group shows at JAM and at Kenkeleba House, a project space on the Lower East Side run by Joe Overstreet and Corinne Jennings that was explicitly dedicated to exhibiting the work of African-American, Latino, Asian-American and Native-American artists. In the summer of 1989, he even had a much-lauded solo exhibition at Exit Art, a pioneering alternative space founded in New York by Jeanette Ingberman and Papo Colo that focused almost entirely on under-represented artists. But one event – a question, actually – seems to have been pivotal in Hammons's crossover from relative obscurity to the mainstream art world. 'How Ya Like Me Now?' was the query, a Kool Moe Dee line the artist emblazoned in spray paint across his billboard-sized depiction of black presidential contender Jesse Jackson as a white-skinned, blue-eyed blond (fig.47). In November 1989, it was installed, at Hammons's bidding, in the empty space between a sidewalk and a parking lot facing the National Portrait Gallery in Washington DC, as his contribution to an exhibition sponsored by the Washington Project for the Arts. No sooner did the piece go up than it was attacked with sledgehammers by several black youths who mistook the critique for a racist insult.[77] The scandal made the news – big time – with *Jet*, the *Los Angeles Times*, *People*, *The International Herald Tribune*, *The New York Times* and a host of other local and international outlets immediately reporting on it. Reverend Jackson himself was asked to weigh in on the affair. But by the time the news sources wanted a quote from the artist, Hammons was already in Europe. No comment. Almost. He spoke to one reporter by phone, and then refused to answer the queries of any other, realizing that the less he said, the more the story would tell itself.[78] And it did.

In the few short years after *How Ya Like Me Now?*, Hammons was catapulted into a new sphere of attention. He was awarded the Prix de Rome for sculpture, with a residency at the American Academy in Rome in 1990. Also that year, he opened a two-part exhibition at Tilton Gallery simultaneous with his first mid-career survey, 'Rousing the Rubble' at P.S.1 Contemporary Art Center in New York, which then travelled to the Institute of Contemporary Art in Philadelphia and the Museum of Contemporary Art San Diego. To accompany the survey, the first monographic catalogue of his work was published.[79] He was invited to take part in landmark group shows in the US and Europe, including 'Places with a Past' (1991) in Charleston, South Carolina, and Documenta IX (1992) in Kassel, Germany. His works were also entering international institutional collections for the first time. In 1991, the French art publication *Galeries Magazine* ran a full-bleed image of him selling snowballs on its cover, while the likes of *Sports Illustrated* and *Newsday* were also reporting on his practice. Accolades accumulated, including one of the most coveted awards conferred in the US, a MacArthur Foundation Fellowship – popularly known as a 'genius grant'. After years of being an outsider to the mainstream art world, Hammons suddenly belonged to a 'new set of stars', as a *New York Times* headline proclaimed.[80]

His art world 'entrance' also signalled an exit of sorts: 'Rousing the Rubble' would be Hammons's first and last major institutional survey. His refusal of most such invitations since has become legendary, with the artist preferring less celebrated venues (at least when it comes to public institutions) and fringe spaces. A wintry Lower East side street corner, an

Illinois state museum with natural history dioramas or a Tribeca shop for ethnic objects – these are apparently more to his liking than any venerable metropolitan art institution or their esteemed biennials (by 1993 Hammons had turned down the Whitney Biennial no less than four times). Marginality, in his case, is willed and dogged, reminding us of bell hooks's theorization of the margins as the ultimate place of resistance.[81] It is a way of not letting the art world and its logic determine the rules of the game. Stanley Whitney puts it well: 'David was very aware of what was going on in the art world and how he was going to really *play* the art world. A lot of people know what they want in the studio and know what they want from their art, but do they know what they want from the art world?'[82]

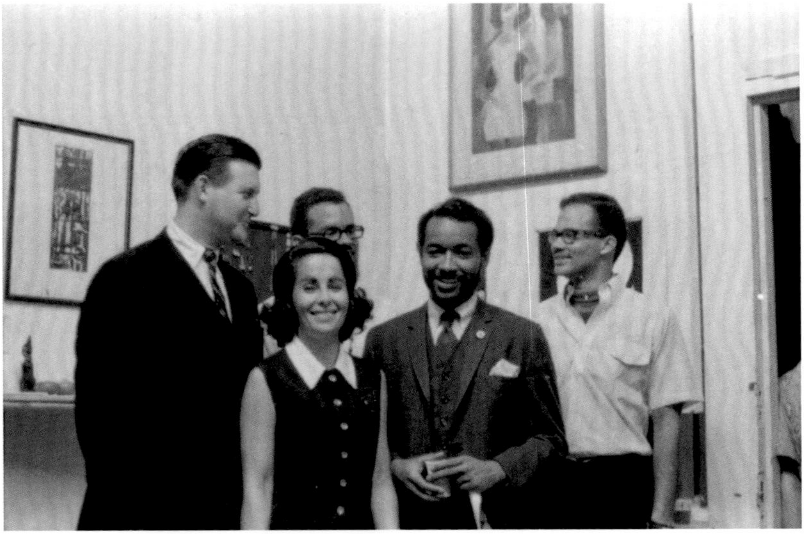

22. Opening at the Brockman Gallery, Los Angeles, c.1968, from left: unknown collectors, Alonzo Davis (behind), David Hammons and Dale Brockman Davis
Courtesy Tilton Gallery, New York

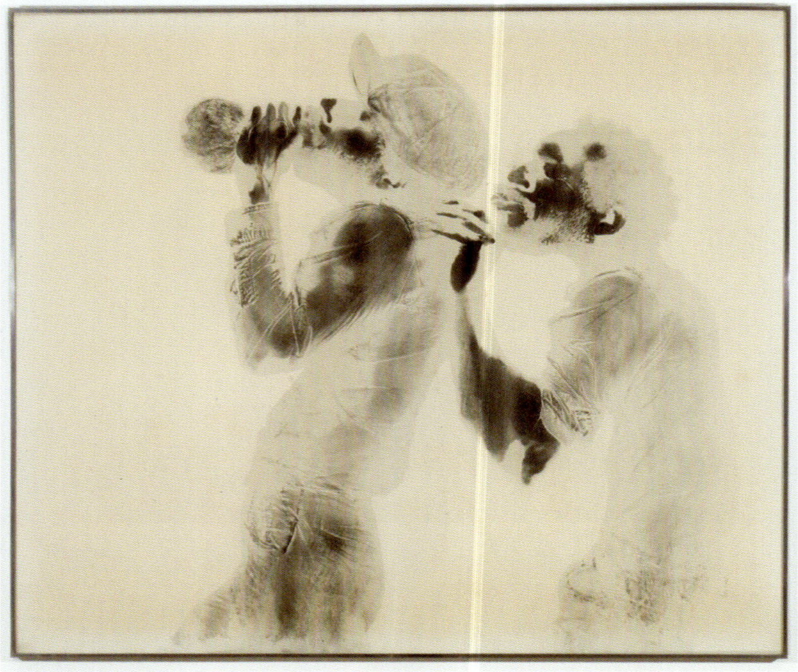

23. David Hammons,
The Wine Leading the Wine, 1969,
body print (margarine and powdered
pigment) on paper,
101.6 × 122.6cm

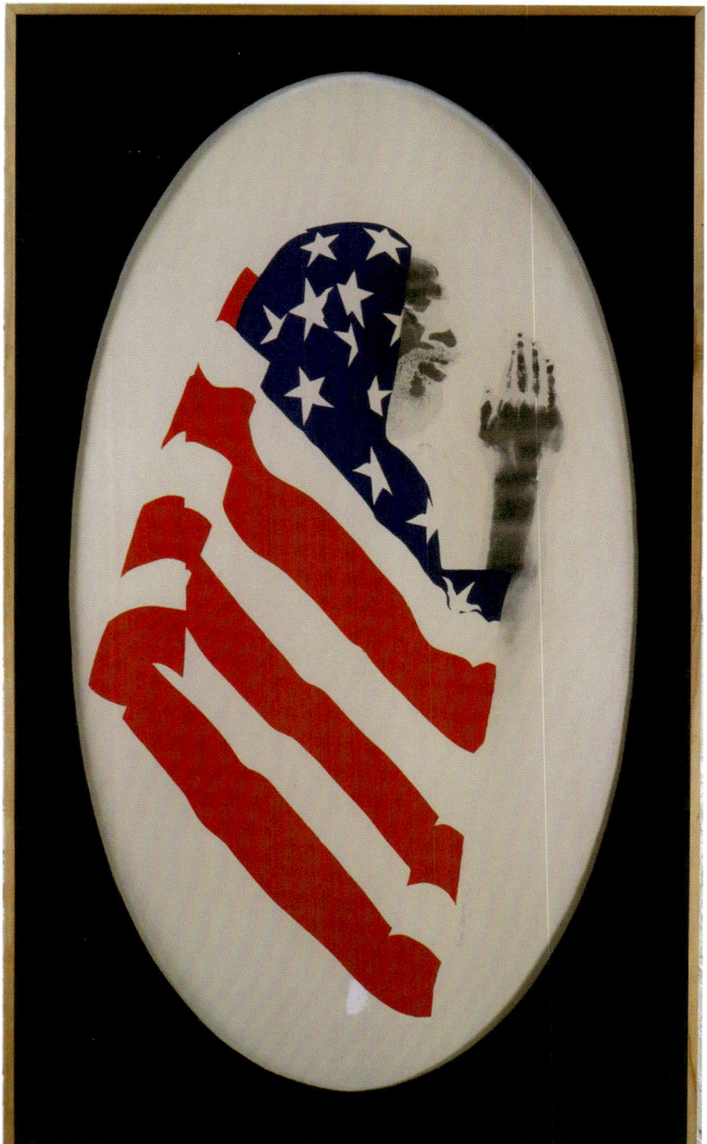

24. David Hammons,
Pray for America, 1969,
body print (margarine and powdered pigment) and sikscreen on paper,
153.7 × 92.7cm

Promised gift to the Museum of Modern Art, New York and the Studio Museum in Harlem by the Hudgins Family in honour of Jack Tilton

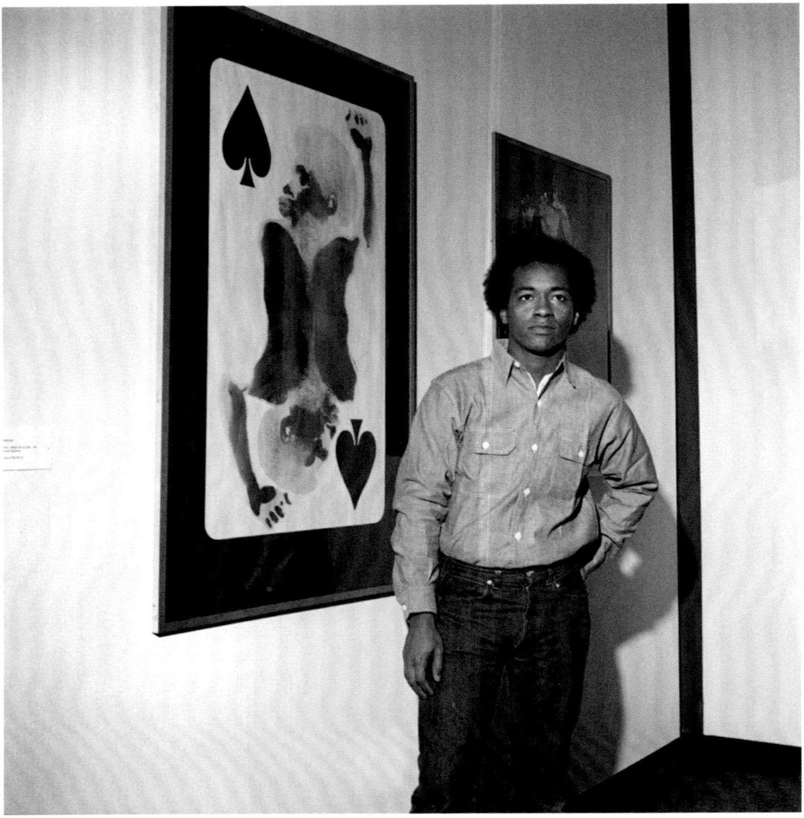

25. David Hammons next to *Spade* (*Power to the Spade*), 1969, body print (margarine and powdered pigment) and silkscreen on paper, 135.3 × 90cm, in 'Three Graphic Artists: Charles White, David Hammons, Timothy Washington', Los Angeles County Museum of Art, 1971. Digital Image © 2022, Museum Associates / LACMA / Art Resource NY / Scala, Florence

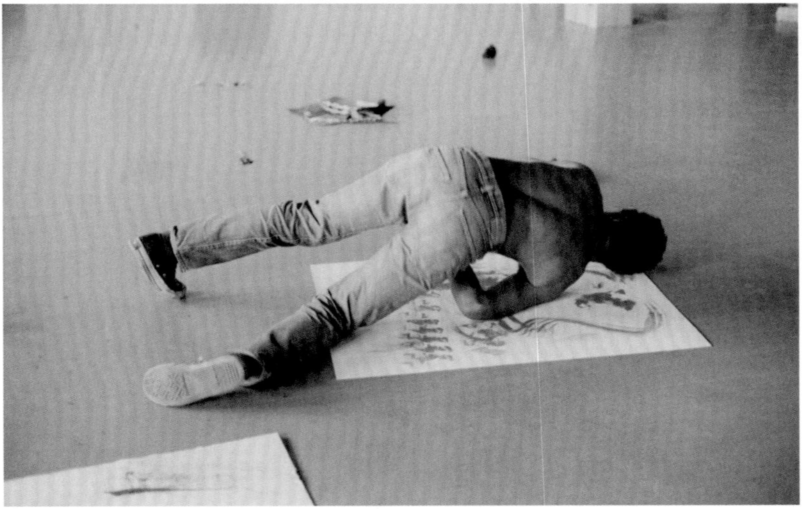

26. David Hammons making body prints,
Slauson Avenue studio, Los Angeles, c.1972
Photograph and courtesy Bruce Talamon

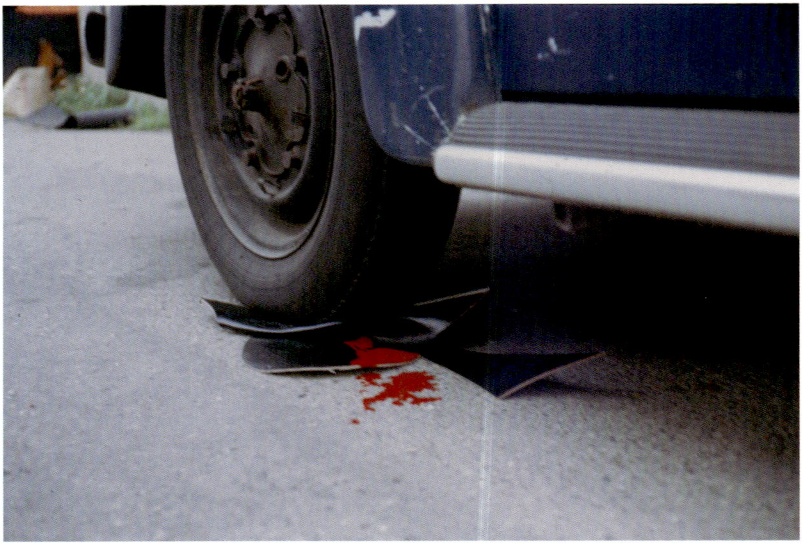

27. Performance view,
David Hammons, *Murder Mystery*,
(also known as *Spade Run Over by a Volkswagen*), 1972, Los Angeles
Courtesy Camille Billops and James V. Hatch Archives at the Stuart A. Rose Manuscript, Archives and Rare Book Library, Emory University, Atlanta

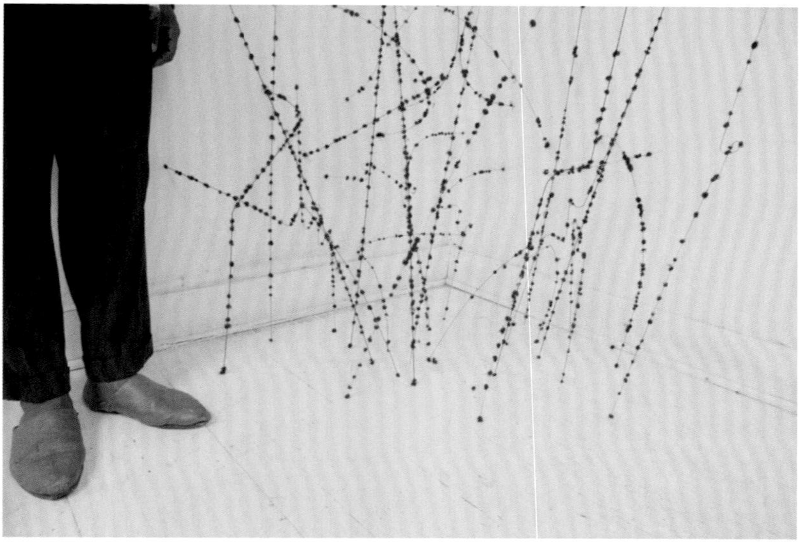

28. David Hammons in his studio with
Hair Garden, Los Angeles, c.1975
Photograph and courtesy Bruce Talamon

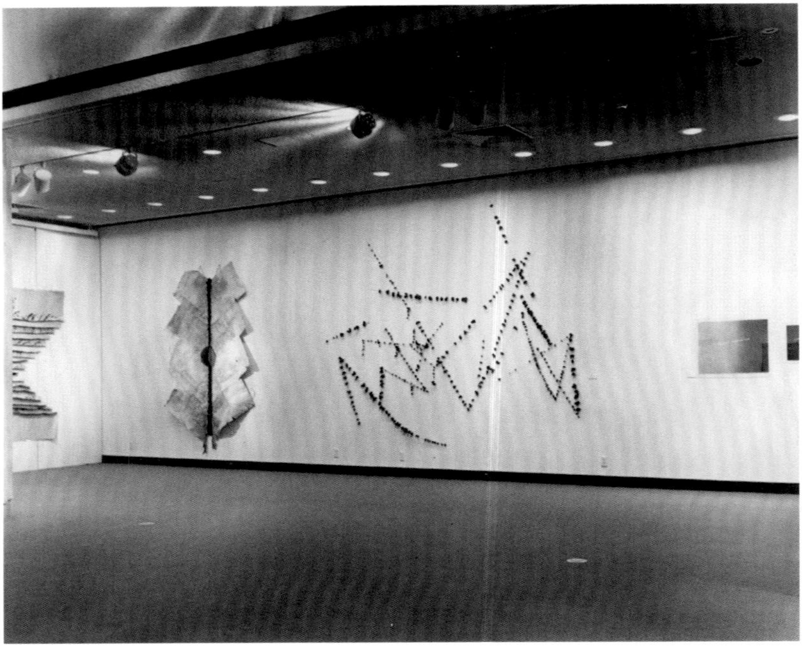

29. Installation view,
David Hammons, *Lady with Bones*
(centre left) and *Untitled (Rubberband*
hair 'drawing') (centre), both 1976,
in 'An Exhibition in Tribute to Dr. Martin
Luther King, Jr.', Los Angeles Municipal
Art Gallery, Barnsdall Park, 1976
Courtesy Tilton Gallery, New York

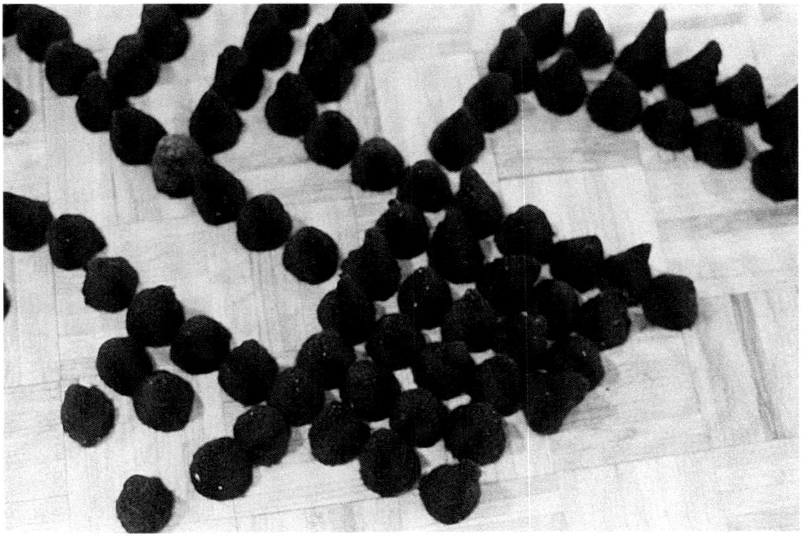

30. Installation view,
David Hammons, *Hair Pyramids*, 1976,
Just Above Midtown, New York, 1976
Courtesy JAM Gallery Archive

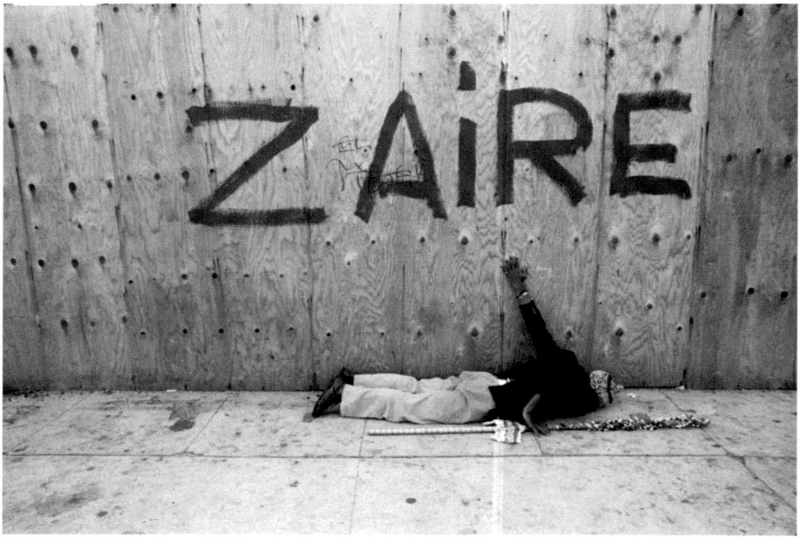

31. Performance view,
David Hammons, *Zaire*, c.1977, Los Angeles
Photograph and courtesy Bruce Talamon

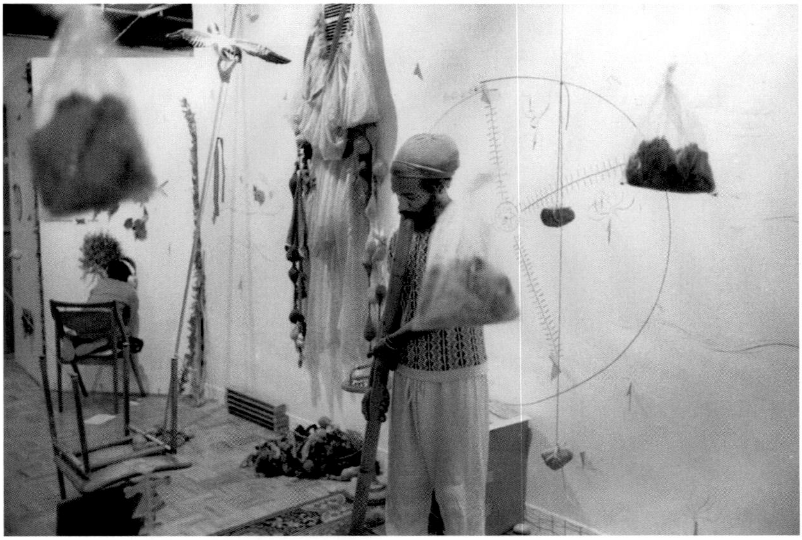

32. David Hammons in residence,
Studio Museum in Harlem, 1981
Photograph and courtesy Frank Stewart

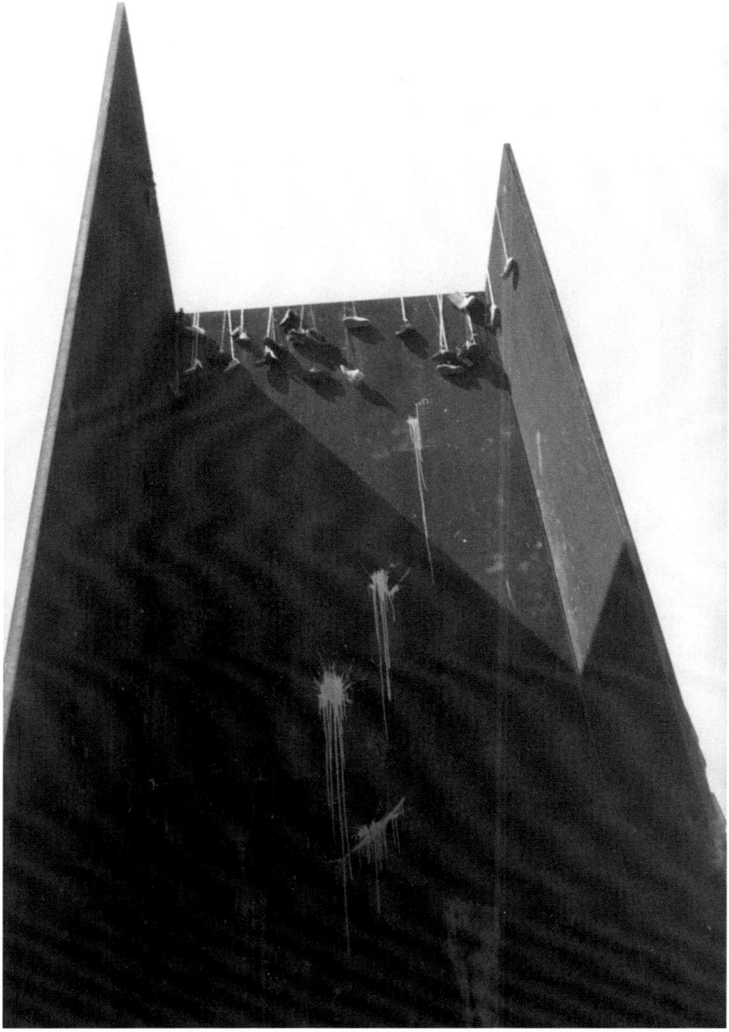

33. David Hammons,
Shoe Tree, 1981, installed on
Richard Serra's *T.W.U.*, 1980,
Franklin Street and West
Broadway, New York
Photograph: Dawoud Bey

Courtesy MoMA P.S.1 Archives,
II.A.794, Museum of Modern Art,
New York. Digital image © 2022,
Photo Scala, Florence/bpk,
Bildagentur fuer Kunst, Kultur
und Geschichte, Berlin

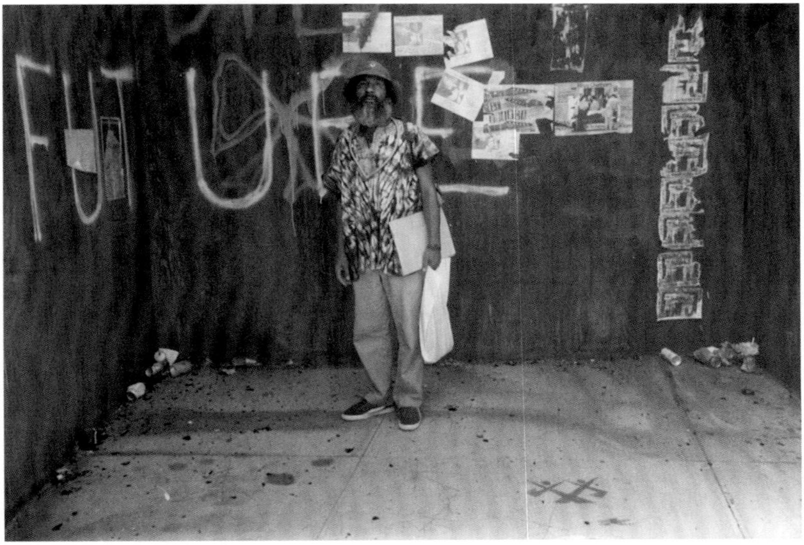

34–37. David Hammons, *Pissed Off*, 1981, performed on Richard Serra's *T.W.U.*, 1980, Franklin Street and West Broadway, New York.
Photographs: Dawoud Bey

34, 36. Courtesy Exit Art Archives, Fales Library and Special Collections, New York University; 35, 37. Courtesy MoMA P.S.1 Archives, II.A.794, Museum of Modern Art, New York. Digital image © 2022, The Museum of Modern Art, New York/Scala, Florence

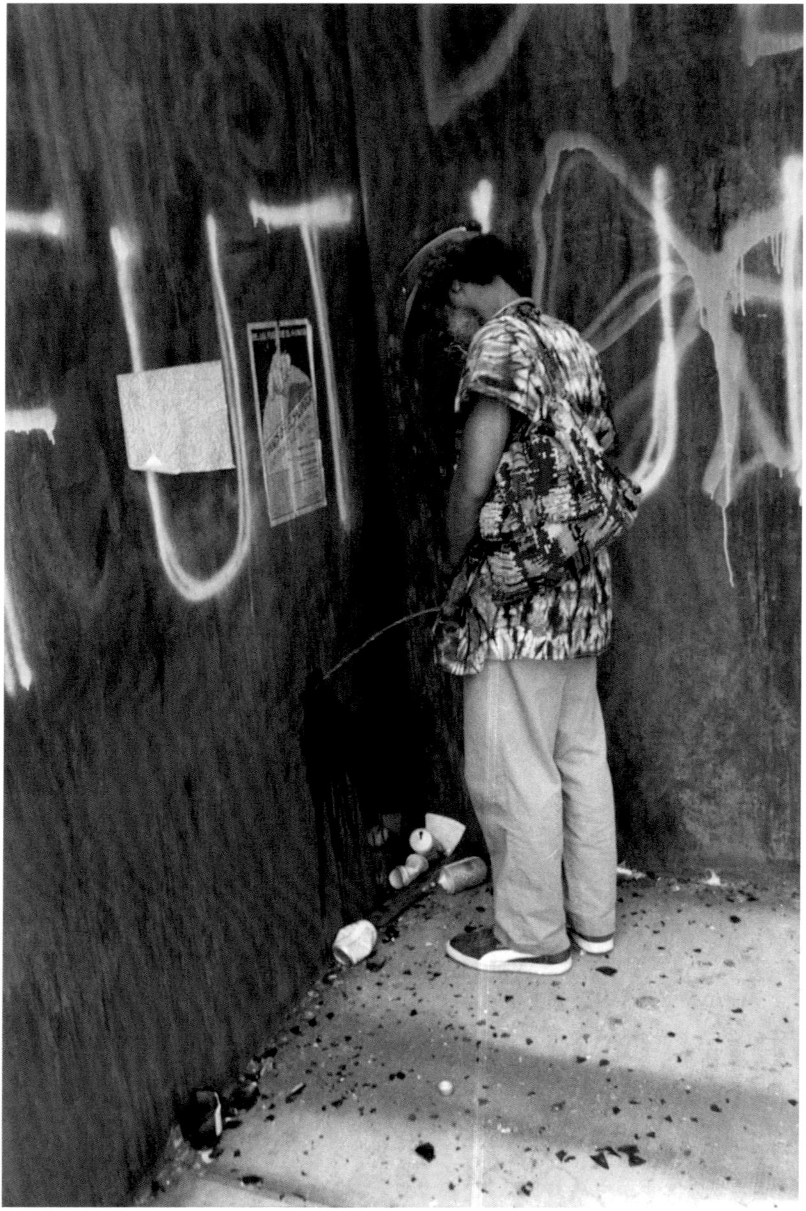

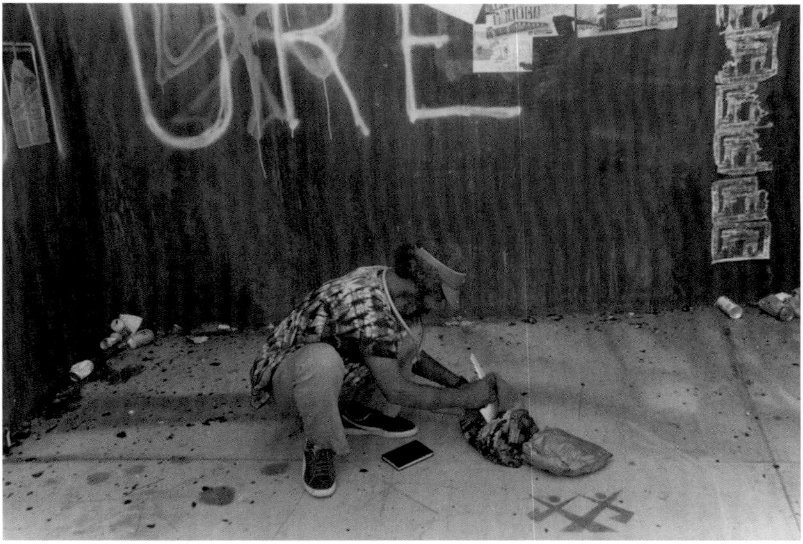

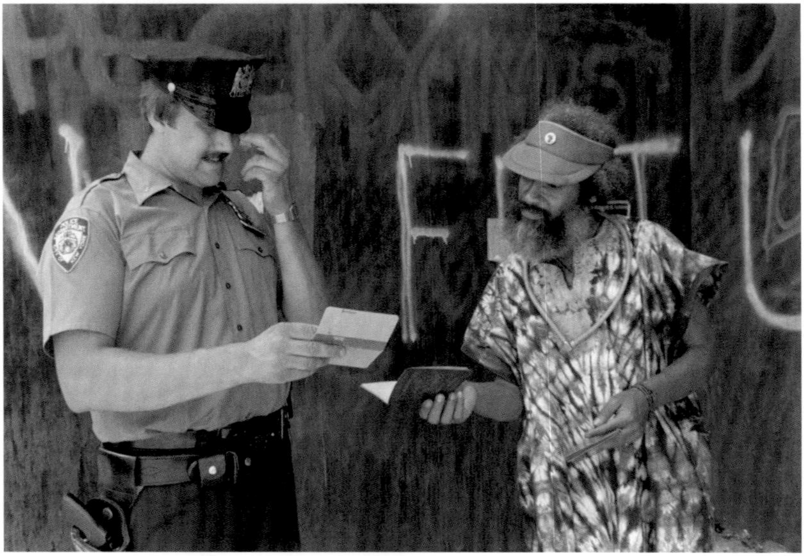

36-37.

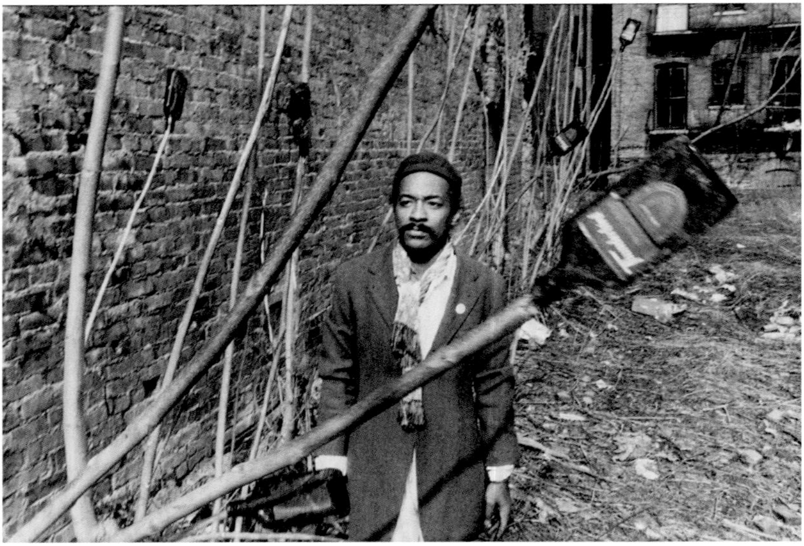

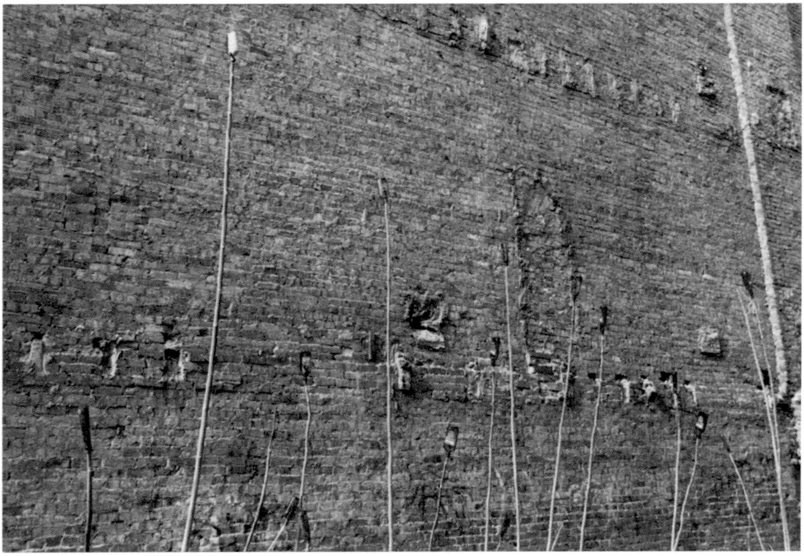

38-39. David Hammons with *Untitled (Bottle Trees)*, c.1982, Harlem
Photographs: Dawoud Bey
Courtesy Exit Art Archives, Fales Library and Special Collections, New York University

Part 3
Stalking *Bliz-aard Ball Sale*

A Blizzard

It was cold in New York City on 13 February 1983. Very cold, in fact. On that second Sunday of the month, the city was recovering from an epic blizzard that had hit the Northeast over several days, leaving a thick blanket of snow. Stores had to muster revenue from previously homebound customers. 'Blizzard Sale!' ads abounded in the local papers: fur coats half off and washing machines at a discount. It was time, Hammons perhaps thought, to have a sale of his own.

He modelled his strategy on that of the street sellers hawking secondhand, maybe trash-plucked findings on the sidewalks around Cooper Square (fig.64). He had observed them regularly, going night after night for years, utterly fascinated by the peddlers' ingenuity and curious aesthetic sense.[83] Consider it research. 'That snowball piece came out of hanging out on Second Avenue all those years, studying all those cats', Hammons has recounted. 'The stuff they'd come up with to sell! One time I saw this cat selling thirty pairs of false teeth! ... I couldn't believe it, two in the morning, he'd be out there with thirty pairs of false teeth. I said, shit, I got to do something like this. So I said, I'm going for the snowballs!'[84]

On that post-blizzard day in February, he created an immaculate setup perfectly positioned between the other regular sellers. As Bey describes it:

> *There was no pre-publicity. It wasn't 'David Hammons' doing a performance. It was a guy selling snowballs. ... It wasn't written up at the time, it wasn't publicized, it wasn't in the* Village Voice, *it wasn't in the art press, nobody sent out a press release. It was for whoever happened to walk by that day. All of his work was about being completely outside the structure and the flow of all of that information. People just encountered it. ... Most people just looked and laughed, they just thought it was so bizarre. And so perfectly comical – a man standing on the street selling snowballs. It wasn't even an Artist on the street, 'cause that would have ruined the effect. It was just a man on the sidewalk selling snowballs.*[85]

But as Robert Farris Thompson has pointed out, there was an aesthetics to Hammons's attention-getting: 'the tantalizing beauty of the pristine spheres, glittering on the textile from North Africa, changed the situation. True, one joker passed by, remarking that he could make his own snowballs, fuck you very much, and didn't need to buy them. But most who did stop stared in fascination.'[86]

What the photographs don't give away, and what remained unsaid about the snowballs for years, was that to make them into perfect globes Hammons used a set of graduated moulds (the kinds often used to shape putty or butter). Found at Canal Plastics, an emporium for all things plastic on Canal Street, the moulds ensured the flawless production of his 'pristine spheres', and helped produce their regimented order: the twenty largest at the top, followed by a row of twelve medium-sized balls, then six smaller ones, twelve just a bit smaller still, six tiny ones, and then six more in the bottommost row, seemingly small enough to melt on contact.

'Can you tell me about making them?' I asked the artist in 2014.

> *I didn't even... Well, there were these two plastic bubble moulds that I used. It was a mould! ... I bought these two moulds out of very thin plastic, each one gets smaller, and slapped the snow between them and they were made. In about three seconds. ... I just made them right there. On the blanket. Uh-huh. I made them very quickly. I mean, I didn't* make *them. There were these half plastic spheres. I don't know what they were for – ceramics, or something.*[87]

Not 'made' at all, according to his telling, but the product of a modest production-line gesture. 'Why not make them by hand?' I wondered. He answered immediately: 'There was no reason to – not once I found these objects down on Canal. ... It was just a concept that however they formed, they formed on their own terms.'[88] Not handmade, then, but not exactly readymade either. Their making was not a performance, and yielded little in the way of obdurate materiality.

Even though Hammons is at pains to insist that the snowballs were 'almost found', their setup – so remarkable in the photographs, so commented on by witnesses – was undeniably *made*. It was carefully composed and very deliberate.[89] A sardonic riff on the serial arrangements of Minimalism,

Hammons's presentation used a Donald Judd–like 'one thing after another' strategy, only to propose its antithesis. Neatly laid out but sitting on an old folded rug on the street, these 'bliz-aard balls' refused to be the authoritative, obdurate, inflexible objects of Minimalism. And it was exactly 'the geometry and precision' of *Bliz-aard Ball Sale*'s staging of snowballs, miming at once the museum's and the supermarket's arrangements, that convinced anyone who saw it that this was 'serious business', as Hammons's friend the photographer Jules Allen recalls.[90]

And, in fact, genuine commerce it was. To insert himself into a context of sales was decisive. Hammons was neither a loner on the street doing a 'performance' (as he once had been in Los Angeles with his street actions) nor was he in a gallery or art-world context, thereby giving the sale the aura of an 'artwork'. As Bey notes:

> *What was important about that location, the side of Cooper Square, is* [...] *that's where people went to sell things if they needed to raise some money* [or] *were desperate to sell something. It was not exactly an open-air market at the time, but the closest thing to that. You could buy everything from a bag of peanuts to secondhand clothes. So, people went there expecting to be able to buy things.*[91]

After the so-called 'dematerialization' of the art object in the 1960s and 70s, when form and matter were said to have been replaced by ideas, systems and documents,[92] or when the object became so spare that its industrial materials and simple, often repeated geometric forms signalled its supposed 'minimalism', the 80s saw a backlash in which the desire for material things returned with a vengeance. Hammons upset all of these tendencies, and constructed the perfect counterproposal to so much of what the art world was then hailing: he obligingly offered customers geometric forms in a choice of sizes and (at least according to some) prices; his were, however, a kind of formalist time bomb, borne from necessarily unstable – melting – material that revealed the perfectly moulded balls as a sly send-up of the serial logic of the commodity and, with it, both Minimalism's dry authority and Conceptual art's immaterial tactics. In this, the snowballs' aesthetic 'perfection' and, indeed, seriality were essential.

The Daringness of the Act

That's why I like doing stuff better on the street, because the art becomes just one of the objects that's in the path of your everyday existence. It's what you move through, and it doesn't have any seniority over anything else.
– David Hammons[93]

To trace Hammons's ephemeral acts and street interventions in the years leading up to *Bliz-aard Ball Sale* is to see how well these anticipated it, mining the street as both inspiration and stage. Sometimes spontaneous (and sometimes not so spontaneous, as the presence of a photographer to document the events suggests), Hammons's performances eschewed the whole art-world machine: official announcements, bona fide institutional spaces and their insider audiences. Instead, he controlled the means of his distribution, constructed his own 'exhibition' context and took his visibility into his own hands.

Over the years of his peregrinations between Los Angeles and New York, Hammons elaborated numerous fleeting and unannounced installations.[94] He erected ephemeral sculptures from wire and hair constellations in his Los Angeles studio (fig.28) but also in the sand along Venice Beach; they were soon after either lost or swept into the dustbin or washed away by the Pacific. And during 1977–78, on a wall in front of a bus stop near Senga Nengudi's studio in South Central LA, he wrote the graffiti 'ZAIRE' (at a moment when the US was helping to quell a 'rebellion' in the former Belgian colony, fig.31), and on another occasion, 'T.V. IS FAKE', then stood or lay beneath the inscription, or sat at the bus stop, watching and waiting. The actions pointed to his political concerns, and attested as well to an art made with, from and, importantly, *for* the streets, with a relative paucity of means and the stimulation of public interaction at its heart. As Nengudi recalls, 'He just sat there, you know. He often does things like that where he'll just in essence "be" and see how people respond to him.'[95]

Then, in 1979, on a vacant lot along a busy Los Angeles street, he reconfigured building detritus in an urban performance, creating a seemingly haphazard, shrine-like installation: 'just moving stones, putting some energy here', as he described it to film-maker Barbara McCullough. In her film, *Shopping Bag Spirits and Freeway Fetishes* (1979), you see Hammons pushing around slabs of discarded concrete and wire, which would be left on the streets to be marvelled at by passers-by or taken to the dump. He was concentrating on the act as much as the resultant object, admitting, 'I'm more concerned with altars right now, which are spirit catchers. But in order to make an altar, you have to perform a ritual.'[96]

In New York, one night in 1981, Hammons made *Pissed Off* ('performed' again seems not quite appropriate here): he urinated on Richard Serra's *T.W.U.* (1980), countering the brute material strength and rigid geometries of the hulking public sculpture with a response at once smelly, formless and furtive. With a title deploying the artist's typical double entendre, *Pissed Off* announced both the sentiment that the Serra piece elicited in Hammons and his bodily reaction. Hammons pissed on the monument and, in an instant, turned it into *his* (Duchampian) urinal. He was not the first to do so: some of the artwork's regular public had been using it as a kind open garbage dump since it was first installed, strewing beer cans and broken glass across the ground in front of it, scrawling graffiti and plastering notices on its steel surface. While Hammons was urinating, a policeman unexpectedly arrived, promptly asking for his ID (fig.34–37). The officer may even have issued a citation, as the story goes, in which case Hammons (would have) trumped Conceptual art's 'aesthetics of administration' with an actual ticket in the NYC Police Department's log (though I myself could not find a trace of it). Even without the ticket, and in perfect Duchampian form, *Pissed Off* was an 'artwork' because Hammons decided it was, with photographs to prove it.

We know all this (much like we 'know' about the *Bliz-aard Ball Sale*) thanks to Bey's photography, his 'clandestine documentation of a non-performance'. Upon seeing the action, and knowing Hammons as he did, Bey knew to 'step back and click'. He had come to Serra's *T.W.U.* at Hammons's goading: 'There's a piece that I made that you don't know about, and probably nobody knows.'[97] The piece in question was in fact *Shoe Tree* (1981, fig.33): over numerous nights, Hammons had thrown about 25 pairs of shoes (tennis shoes mostly, but also work boots, rubber galoshes and at least one pair of women's high heels), tied together by shoe laces, onto the top edges of the 36-foot-tall, 72-tonne Corten steel plates of Serra's homage to the Transport Workers Union.[98] The dangling shoes – scuffed, dirty and shambolically 'displayed' – gave the monument curves and made it softer, more human, according to Hammons.[99] It also made Serra's imposing work into a mere pedestal for Hammons's sculpture, a holder of his shoes.

A pair of shoes connected by their laces and flung over a power line has long been a vernacular prevalent in American cities even if cryptic to those outside its 'lexicon'. Signal of a drug den or marker of gang sprawl, trace of a bully's actions or celebration of the end of the school year: suspended shoes mean different things depending on the place, but common to them all is the announcement of territorial conquest, the statement of personal agency in public space. This also applied to *Shoe Tree*. Flinging shoes on *T.W.U.* was a means of claiming an unruly urban folk tradition to unseat and disrupt the formidable (white) art world.

It is impossible to know how long Hammons's family of shoes dangled there, or how many people noticed. Or to know, indeed, if the shoe 'assemblage' was found by officials and removed before *T.W.U.* itself was disassembled on 30 July 1981 (the sculpture's installation in lower Manhattan was fated from the start to be temporary). Serra himself was, it is said, upset about Hammons's intervention; he considered it a defamation of his artwork, even though he, like most people, didn't know who was responsible for it at the time. Only years later did a single photograph by Bey of *Shoe Tree* (taken after the photographer discovered the piece during the making of *Pissed Off*) begin to circulate; it was a subtle announcement of Hammons as the 'author'.

Even if he was *Shoe Tree*'s maker, here and elsewhere Hammons opened the 'authoring' of an artwork to a wider, non-art public via gestures that rhymed with popular, demotic activities: kids throwing sneakers over telephone wires or pissing on 'public' art. And if the monument temporarily became 'a Hammons' (and no longer 'a Serra'), or indeed could be said to have been 'made' by a still wider public, we might also ask, *when* and *where* is the 'artwork'? I ask this because activities that took either no permanent material form or a negligible one, and that were built from preexisting materials (in this case, ostensibly someone else's art), are vital to understanding Hammons's practice – perhaps even more so than any of his lasting, collection-worthy pieces. He himself has admitted: 'It's not the art object itself. It's the daringness of the act, of presenting it, and the art object is the result ... of empowering the object, as opposed to the object being powerful.'[100]

Could it be, then, that you have to entirely recalibrate your reading of Hammons's art so as to understand it not in terms of objects but in terms of the 'empowering' acts that bring them into being? After all, so much of what he does simply would never enter into art history were we to speak only of the enduring, clear-cut and 'proper' objects that remain of his practice. Still, you might wonder when, exactly, pieces such as *Shoe Tree, Pissed Off* and *Bliz-aard Ball Sale* came to constitute artworks at all. Was it when the piece was made or in the moment Bey documented it; the moment Hammons gave it a title, perhaps after some contemplation, or when he allowed its photographic trace to circulate? And maybe the documentation of *Pissed Off* is a re-enactment of sorts, recording an act that Hammons, in fact, performed at every opportunity he had: throw a shoe on the Serra and piss on it; return the next day. While a handful of friends may have been in the know, the wider public likely dismissed these pieces as mere pranks or acts of vandalism, only to become aware of them as art when their respective titles, dates, attribution and evidential record circulated, often years after the fact.[101]

As of 1981, Hammons began intermittently making his 'bottle trees', for which he threaded the bare branches of ailanthus trees in the vacant lots across from his studio and next to the Studio Museum in Harlem with upturned empty wine bottles (fig.38–39). Those trees, known as 'poverty trees' or 'ghetto palms' for their capacity to thrive in urban wastelands, were ubiquitous in unclaimed niches of Harlem. The bottles Hammons added to them were easy to collect, plentiful as they were in local alleyways and at street corners, especially since the artist preferred the cheapest sorts. (Thunderbird and Night Train, at 86 cents a bottle, were the urban poor's brands of choice.)[102] With these, he created his own form of Kongo *minkisi*, adapting a tactic used to ward off evil spirits by catching them in the 'flash' of the glass.[103] In the process, he mixed a commentary on the fate of downtrodden drunks with the strange elegance of a vodou ritual – at sites decidedly outside of the art world's circuit or logic. In a move that anticipated some of the strategies that would be vital to *Bliz-aard Ball Sale*, Hammons's bottle trees were ephemeral, installed without label or fanfare, and meant for whomever happened upon them.[104]

By 1982, he had erected a predecessor to his *Higher Goals* (1983) – bedazzling, improbably high basketball hoops – on one of these same vacant lots in Harlem. He installed the first of the poles just across from his Harlem studio.[105] He then installed another one, even taller, in 1983, just near it, at West 121st Street and Frederick Douglass Boulevard, not long after realizing *Bliz-aard Ball Sale* (fig.41–42). It comprised 16.8 metres of utility poles nailed and wired together with a decorated hoop at the top. These were works of public art in the most fundamental sense, installed in unused urban space and made for a 'public' Hammons knew and lived amongst, created at the artist's own initiative and drawing upon a 1982 National Endowment for the Arts project grant, but without the invitation or sanction of any official 'public space' commission. People in the neighbourhood recognized him from it and stopped him to talk about it; it acted, he says, like his 'calling card' long thereafter.[106]

Hammons produced a grouping of five more in 1986, each pole adorned with thousands of bottle caps arranged in geometric patterns, often following African motifs (fig.45–46). Commissioned by New York City's Public Art Fund, they were installed for a short time as a group on Cadman Plaza in Downtown Brooklyn. These in turn inspired others, made from junkyard scraps (car windows as backboards, bottomless plastic pails as hoops) and meant to be displayed indoors. As with so much of his work, Hammons got the idea for them from the basketball hoops in Harlem that had been jury-rigged to play a sport often thought of as one of the few ways for black youth to escape poverty. There was a hoop on his block made from U-clamps and two-by-fours attached to a pole, and once he had seen it, he began to notice others in the neighbourhood made from materials that were simply at hand – from paper bags and cardboard boxes to wooden crates.[107]

Observation of the streets binds much of Hammons's work. The very year he made *Bliz-aard Ball Sale*, Hammons applied for a grant by explaining his proposal in a single sentence that requested funding to travel to the South simply 'to look at black people' – at the things they make and the way they live. He got the grant.[108] In privileging the act of looking over the production of permanent objects, this funding proposal illustrates that his attention to the codes and mores of the street – whether in the American South, Harlem or on the Lower East Side – is the very foundation of his working method.

This method is central to *Bliz-aard Ball Sale*. In order to make the piece, Hammons spent countless nights watching other street sellers, and once he had set up his own meticulous display, the whole of his action entailed positioning himself, back to the wall, to see how potential customers reacted to his inventory. With a truculence and humour that has become his mainstay, he was watching the streets, but also attempting to speak to them.

When you have an object between you and them, people will talk to you. They'll say, 'What is that? Is that for sale?' But if you're just standing on a street corner, everyone's an enemy of each other. But one object... it becomes a conduit for conversation with someone you've never met before.[109]

Fugitive Evidence

The work we know as *Bliz-aard Ball Sale* probably didn't bear that title, or any title at all, when it took place. It just *was*. When exactly it acquired a name and how many alternative titles there may have been before this one can only be a matter of conjecture. At some point between 1983–89, a postcard was produced from one of Bey's images of the sale, cropping out a neighbouring vendor to show only a jovial Hammons leaning against a wall with his snowballs arranged before him. 'Street Vendor Selling Snowballs / Performance by David Hammons, 1983 / Photograph by Dawoud Bey' is printed on the back (fig.65–66).[110] Did Hammons make this and other such postcards sometime after the action to circulate to friends and acquaintances, so as to quietly spread news of his action? Or did he, as Linda Goode Bryant jokingly speculates, have plans to slip them among the ubiquitous postcard racks that tourists regularly bought from?[111] Whatever its purpose, whatever its destination, based on this postcard we can conclude that *Bliz-aard Ball Sale* was not yet the name of what is pictured at the time of its making. Indeed, some of Bey's early photographic prints of the sale – found amidst the preparatory material for a catalogue that was never published – have 'Street Vendor' or 'Street Vendor Selling Snowballs' scribbled on the back.[112] One such photograph, printed and annotated just a couple of years after the sale, bears that latter elucidation crossed out with 'Blizzard Art Sale' added (fig.67). One can chalk this up to hasty imprecision, or perhaps Hammons hadn't thought to title the work at the time or even in the years immediately after. He probably hadn't thought of it at all until his 1990 exhibition at P.S.1, where, on the backs of the photographs collected in the preparation of the show (fig.68), and some of which were published in the accompanying catalogue, the 'official' title was announced for the first time in print: *Bliz-aard Ball Sale.*

Bey had been called in for the occasion and asked to record the project. Two sets of his images of the sales event exist, in black-and-white and colour slide film. They suggest preparation. Effort. They suggest, in fact, that any understanding of Hammons's practice as a whole – and *Bliz-aard Ball Sale* in particular – must attend to a complex relationship to photography. Such attention to documentation would need to concern itself with Hammons's seemingly irreconcilable strategies of cultivating evasion *and* regularly commissioning an evidential record.

Throughout Hammons's career, photography has occupied a vital if ambiguous place. He has befriended numerous professional photographers – Bey, of course, but also Jules Allen, Danny Dawson, Erma Estwick, Ari Marcopoulos, Ellen Page Wilson, Bruce Talamon, Frank Stewart and Coreen Simpson, among others – and he has engaged them over the years to record his ephemeral actions. He's known to have called them up with little notice (along the lines of 'Hey, I'm doing something, want to come over?'), or just showed up at their apartments with his assemblages to be photographed.[113] Often, the photographers were the first public for his artworks. And sometimes an ephemeral assemblage would not survive except for the photograph of it, making the image its sole vehicle of public dissemination.

Likely countless actions by Hammons escaped documentation, and deliberately so. We can't know how many nor what they actually were. From arranging to have several photographers gather to click their camera flashes at the same time under his direction in 1981, to tossing up handfuls of rice grains outside a locked-up church that he passed one night in 2002, to ceremoniously offering Brussels sprouts on the stalk to those who dared meet him at a specified street corner in 2010, the tales of unpredictable and undocumented actions by the artist circulate as urban legend. And then suddenly, inexplicably, he will orchestrate the recording of an action.

When, in 1972, he drove a Volkswagon over leather spades, he made sure his red-paint-splattered scraps were documented (fig.27). When, a few years later, he installed a wire and hair work in the corner of his Los Angeles studio, he had Bruce Talamon photograph him caught with his feet in their midst (*Hair Garden*, 1975). When he threw shoes onto Serra's *T.W.U.* in 1981, he dressed in white coveralls for the part and had it videotaped, even before he had Bey photograph the 'finished' *Shoe Tree.* When he installed *Pole Dreams* in 1982, the predecessor to his improbably high basketball hoops, he organized a procession through Harlem, complete with face paint and feathers for the participants, and asked journalist Gylbert Coker to take part while Coreen Simpson recorded it on camera (fig.40).[114] When, in 1990, he crafted a finger puppet from his gloved hand and a photographic cut-out of prize fighter Joe Louis, he had Bey document it before he titled it *St. Louis* (fig.53). When he took a rock covered with African-American hair for styling in a Harlem barbershop, he had the 1992 act, titled *Haircut* (fig.55), both filmed and photographed by Simpson and Ari Marcopoulos, and made sure poet John Farris was also there so that he could later write about it. Even if no photographic documents have become as iconic, or circulated as widely, as the images of *Bliz-aard Ball Sale*, these other actions have lived on precisely because they have been attributed, titled, documented and disseminated.

'Art history', André Malraux once declared, 'is the history of that which can be photographed.'[115] Hammons understood this from the start. As Nengudi says of the role of photography for Hammons and other African-American artists like herself working in the 1970s and 80s, documenting what they were doing was critical to proving their very existence; their activities, they knew well, were not likely to be recorded for wider art histories.[116] For the 'long game' that Hammons freely admits to playing, photography performs a key role. *Bliz-aard Ball Sale*'s very existence and iconic status in the history of art is warranted – and even *constructed* – by its affiliation with photography; in other words, by its relationship to documentation.

And yet, as important as these photographs evidently are, Hammons has systematically let them circulate primarily as cheap reproductions. In the wake of both photo-conceptualism and the documentation of early performance art, Hammons refused to treat *Bliz-aard Ball Sale*'s photographs (or any of his work's photographs) as equivalent to the ephemeral object/performance, and he seems to have never exhibited or sold them *as* artworks. They have not been certified, signed or traded as the somehow authentic indexical trace of the artwork in the way that similar documentation has been by so many of his predecessors. Instead, over the years, the photographs of Hammons's *Bliz-aard Ball Sale* that were put into circulation have become mass-reproduced representations of an absent auratic original: magazine, internet and slide images deflecting preciousness and art-world snobbishness, offering no clear artistic or commodity status.[117]

Given that the photographs of *Bliz-aard Ball Sale* didn't enter into public or private collections as stand-ins for the artwork, and that no other material traces remain, what exactly, you might ask, entered history?

One answer is: secondhand stories backed up by magazine and catalogue photographs. Indeed, an understanding of the action has been formed by the photographic – by a few now-iconic images of the sale – which in turn has inflected the stories (of those who actually saw it, those who think they saw it and those who know they didn't but somehow feel they nevertheless 'know' it because they know its documentation).

Temporary Business Ventures

Play the game, but don't believe in it – that much you owe yourself. ... Play the game, but raise the ante, my boy. Learn how it operates, learn how you operate.
– Ralph Ellison[118]

'I sold 'em 'cause I knew that people couldn't hold 'em', Hammons once said of his snowballs.[119] That 'defined David's work at that particular moment', Bey notes, 'the fact that no one will ever own *Bliz-aard Ball Sale*. There's nothing to own.'[120] Hammons underscored this, declaring it a life principle:

> *There's no 'I bought him'. There's no object in the transaction. No one can say, 'I've got a David Hammons on my wall, you're invited over for dinner to see my latest purchase.' I'm not into that. I'll dabble in it, but I'm not in it exclusively in that European way of art as commodity.*[121]

Different from how either 'European' art flaunted its commodity status or how Conceptual art conceived of itself *contra* commodification, Hammons deliberately constructed the conditions for his art to become critical of the entire transformation of the object into traded goods by emphasizing the transubstantiation of one into the other. And whereas Marcel Broodthaers may have declared that the 'definition of artistic activity occurs, first of all, in the field of distribution',[122] Hammons wagers that, more specifically, it lies in the *transaction*.

Not only has he made a life work of resuscitating the trash and ruins of capitalist dereliction, Hammons has also repeatedly adopted the so-called black market as his model. Creating various temporary business ventures, he makes the commercial transaction – or even specifically the illicit commercial transaction, a hustle, in other words – his cardinal medium. The transaction is not only a means for the artwork's distribution, but sometimes an artwork in and of itself. There are models for this. Duchamp is perhaps the most obvious, as he not only created works that performatively addressed speculative value, including his *Tzanck Check* (1919) and *Monte Carlo Bond* (1924), but was, throughout his life, a quasi-dealer of his own and others' works, 'cheerfully masquerading as an American-style "businessman"', as his first biographer put it.[123] So it is with Hammons – the businessman masquerade, that is. (It also hardly comes as surprise that when Hammons recently bought a property in Yonkers, New York, where it is rumoured he plans to start his own museum, he registered it in the name of Duchamp Realty LLC.)[124]

If Duchamp's readymade took a found object of mass production and attempted to insert it into an aesthetic realm, thereby shining a light on the fraught mechanics of both exchange value and exhibition value, Hammons takes nothing more than frozen water and sells it on a bustling New York street corner, rejecting art institutions and their discernment of value altogether (insisting instead on the frosty object's use-value, to be literally *used*, as snowballs usually are). Hammons did this in the face of a 1980s art market overrun with the circulation of exchange value; he was creating something valuable 'in its disruption of valuation, in its radical unbankability', to use the words of Fred Moten.[125] Thus, for all his willed affinity with Duchamp, by putting snowballs into circulation outside the studio, beyond the reach of galleries and museums, curators and collectors, Hammons traced a very different trajectory. But even if the realms into which the two artists inserted their objects were diametrically opposed, there is a correlation: in the snowball sale, much as in the display and circulation of the readymade, the 'object' is inseparable from what could be called its *curation*, that is, the ways in which Hammons positioned, mediated and publicized his action and its objects.[126] As with Duchamp's *Fountain* of 1917, the mechanisms of display, promotion and photographic and testimonial circulation at work in *Bliz-aard Ball Sale* and, just as importantly, its ability to evade or *delay* a certain kind of capture, are arguably as much the artwork as the snowballs themselves.

The phenomenon of the artist as sales agent was not entirely new. Martha Rosler, for instance, in 1973 set up a monumental 'garage sale' and sold off her personal belongings in the museal confines of the University Art Gallery, University of California, San Diego. Hammons instead ensconced himself in the shadow economy of the street, confusing his wares/works with regular commodities. His was arguably also a more insidious approach than that of Claes Oldenburg, who in 1961 created *The Store* in an empty Lower East Side storefront. Oldenburg's display and sale of quasi-formless representations of cupcakes, rib-eye steaks and girdles was rooted in the premise that all art, no matter how recalcitrant, no matter how avant-gardist or daring, is recuperable by middle-class culture.[127] His intent – and this could just as well apply to Hammons's hawking of snowballs at Cooper Square – was to skip over the illusory stage in which art pretends to escape commodification. Hammons, for his part, decided that rather than simulating a site of commerce, he would infiltrate one. This was the point made by Duchamp's insertion of himself at the Concours Lépine, an inventors fair in Paris where, positioned among vendors peddling vegetable slicers and garbage compressors, he attempted (unsuccessfully) to sell his *Rotoreliefs* in 1935.

But if Rosler or Oldenburg or Duchamp may have offered models of the artist-as-salesperson, Hammons for his part set out his stall and deliberately played at being a hustler of the most disreputable type. The quasi-illicit context of a site for unauthorized street selling was crucial to him. On that corner, the vendors would probably have gathered up their goods and disappeared if an unforgiving cop came by. Hammons suggested that not only does art not escape commodification, it doesn't escape being a con job. 'What, after all', one critic noted, 'could be more of a scam than selling snowballs in winter?'[128]

Bliz-aard Ball Sale was not his only street-side sales act. Describing the circumstances of a set of sales he held between 1985–87, of white, rubber shoes for dolls, Hammons told a critic: 'A friend gave me 10,000 pairs of tiny rubber shoes. And I've been selling them in Cooper Square. Fifty cents a foot. I tell the ladies, "If you buy these shoes, he'll never walk out of your life."'[129] He sold them all summer long, for three summers, he attests. There was an art to the daily changing display, and witnesses recall the complexity and seemingly infinite variations of his presentations. Hammons himself has admitted that he deliberately created 'intricate patterns', his display a veritable aesthetic statement. But again, the sale decidedly wasn't for the art world: 'If I see a member of the art crowd coming, I jump behind a door.'[130] Though repeatedly staged but apparently never photographically recorded or officially titled, the sale of the doll shoes was intimately connected to *Bliz-aard Ball Sale*, the two constituting, by Hammons's own account, his 'personal best'.[131]

It was important to him that he look convincing and that people might actually *buy* the goods at his various sales. Hammons urged friends who might have spied him not to linger too long, for he didn't want them to ruin his credibility as a salesman.[132] And as Corinne Jennings puts it:

> *He would pretend he was a regular trader.* [He] *dressed like the other traders, and he didn't want to be acknowledged, he wanted to be treated like a trader, which is what he was out there doing. He was selling crazy stuff, you know? So* [to not] *give away his identity, I had to become a customer.*[133]

Robert Farris Thompson traces the roots of Hammons's shoe sales, like the artist's other works involving clothing, to his upbringing in proximity to the secondhand garments in his foster-grandfather Claude Champ's thrift shop.[134] Perhaps this is the origin of those sales, and the artist's fly sartorial style in general. I cannot help but read in it the origins of Hammons's *trading* – the act of taking unwanted things and trying to make money from their re-contextualization, presentation and sale. The transaction sits at the heart of Hammons's 'performances' at Cooper Square and, indeed, much of his life work. One friend who saw him selling the shoes admits: 'I know that I was appalled at his prices. [*laughs*] For shoes that were not real!'[135] Questioned regarding those prices, witnesses' memories are vague. But as one insists, 'There was always some kind of exchange. You couldn't have them for free. ... [With David] there was *always* an exchange.'[136]

The Colour of Money

'I'm not working that hard', Hammons once proclaimed. 'When you find a found object, the work is halfway complete because the object is talking to you. Whereas everything at [the art supply store] Pearl Paint is devoid of spirit; you have to bring everything to it.'[137] But his was no cynical derision of the artwork borne of effort; and certainly, some of his early works involved great exertion (think of the collecting and nailing of thousands of bottle caps for *Higher Goals*). Rather, at a certain moment his refusal to work hard became a matter of strategy and statement: 'I'm not going to put that much energy into an art object to prove to these folks that I'm legitimate. I did it once. But now that I'm not going to spend like, uh, the rest of my life overworking, like James Brown, the hardest working man, he up sweatin' and screamin' and crawlin' on the floor to prove to these folks that you're a good singer. I'm not gonna do this shit.'[138] Indeed, why sweat?

Perceptions of race, Hammons knows, often are forged through details. For instance, the overextension of effort supposed to act as evidence of (black) talent and as currency to attain normative (white) privilege. Maybe that's why he has championed the slight but transfixing gesture, for example, of *Bliz-aard Ball Sale*. After all, what could be more simple *and less work* than making snowballs in winter? With his store-bought mould, he didn't even need to 'make' them at all, he insists. But because of that, what could be more challenging than ensuring that the snowballs and their display look remarkable, worthy of remembering – mythical even?

While his way of working may appear ad hoc, it is never slapdash. 'Simply built, but not simply conceived', as Tom Finkelpearl, curator of Hammons's exhibition 'Rousing the Rubble', points out.[139] Those who know Hammons describe not only his restless, unrelenting energy in making things, but also his incredible seriousness and care: it can take a long time for a mere found object to be transformed into an artwork worthy of the designation. For instance, the rock you see on the floor in a circa 1991 photograph of his studio could take years before being either ultimately rejected or coiffed with some of the collected hair in the barrel near his window to become part of the *Rock Head* series (fig.54).[140] This gravitas – perhaps so unexpected that it is little written about – is surely what gives Hammons's process and the resultant works their peculiar profundity.

It was no different with *Bliz-aard Ball Sale*. It took years of studying street sellers before he decided to sell his own snowballs, even if his sale hinged on the modest economy of its making (as does most all of Hammons's work). A certain consciousness, not monetary investment, made his works what they were. As he once noted:

> *You know, I used to go to these Black art colonies, and they used to like, destroy me! You know all those cats saying, 'My shit's about Madonna and child, the solar system, another sun coming up, the universe is the Black man' … and I'm talking about making art out of ice cubes!* [laughs] *Man, I'm talking about Black folks buying $200 worth of paper to make art on. And then they're*

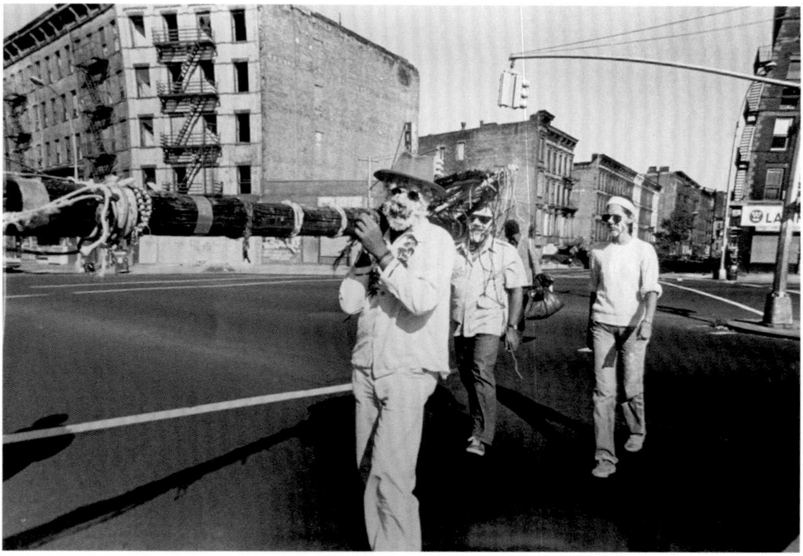

40. Performance view,
David Hammons, *Human Pegs / Pole Dreams*, 1982, Harlem
Photograph and courtesy Coreen Simpson

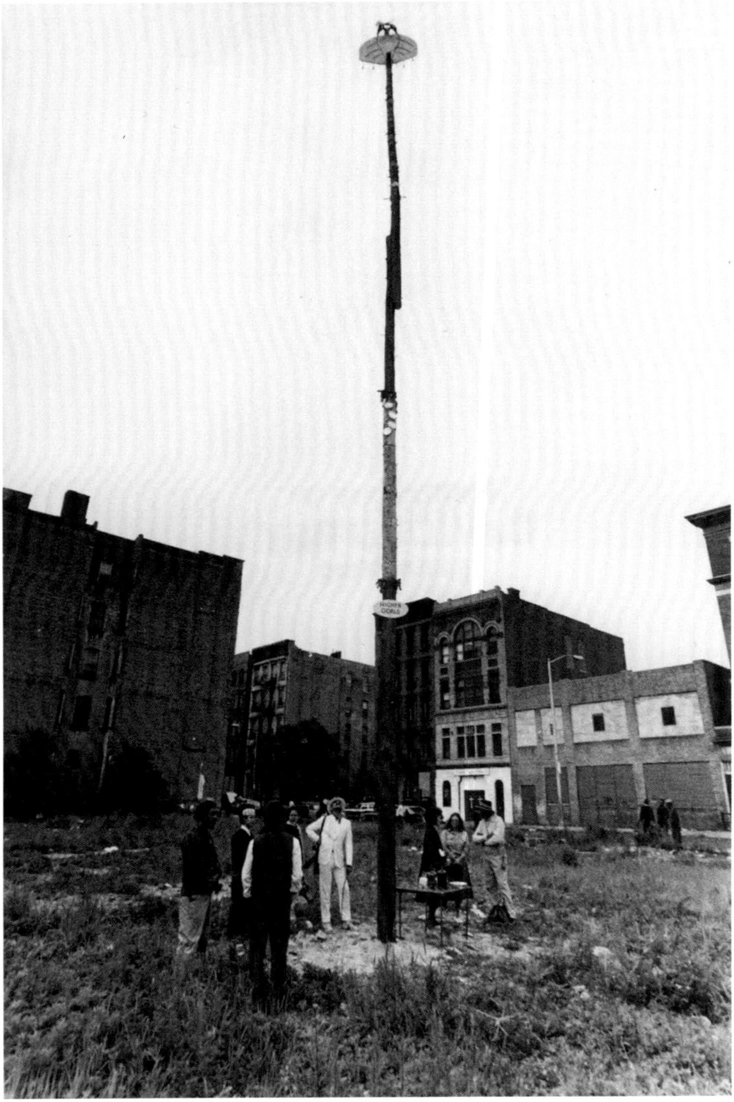

41. David Hammons,
Higher Goals, 1983,
16.8m basketball poles,
121st Street and Frederick Douglass
Boulevard, Harlem
Photograph: Dawoud Bey

Courtesy Exit Art Archives, Fales Library
and Special Collections, New York
University

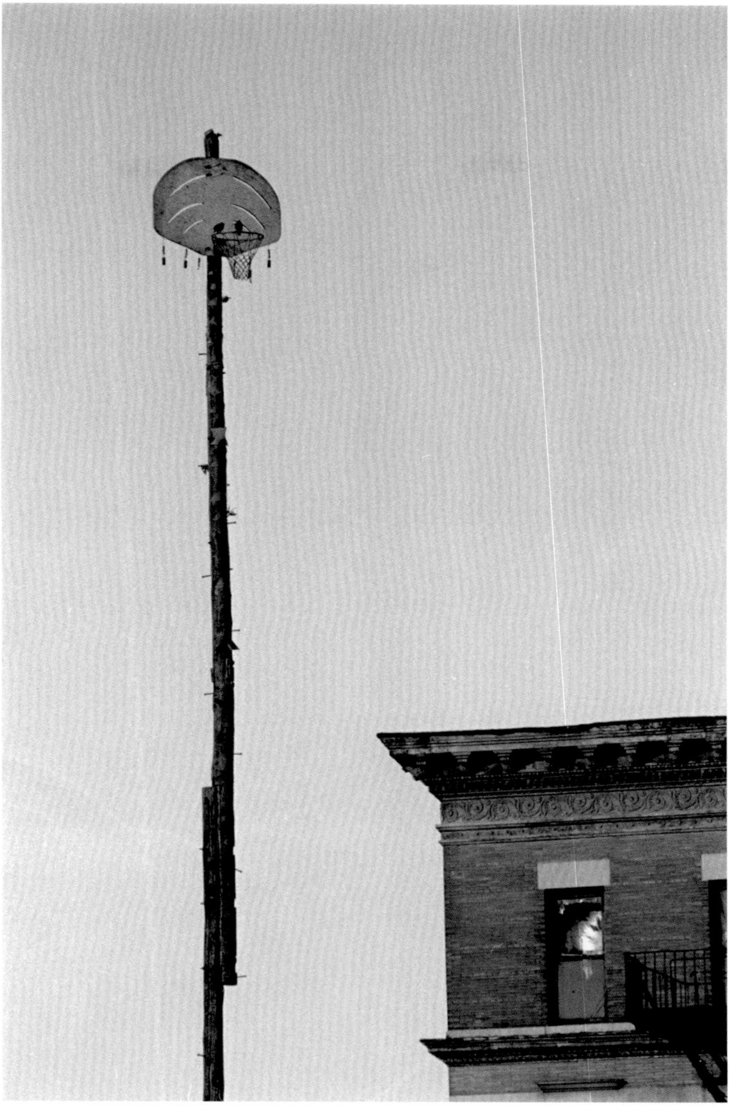

42. David Hammons,
Higher Goals, 1983,
16.8m basketball poles,
121st Street and Frederick Douglass
Boulevard, Harlem
Photograph and courtesy Matt Weber

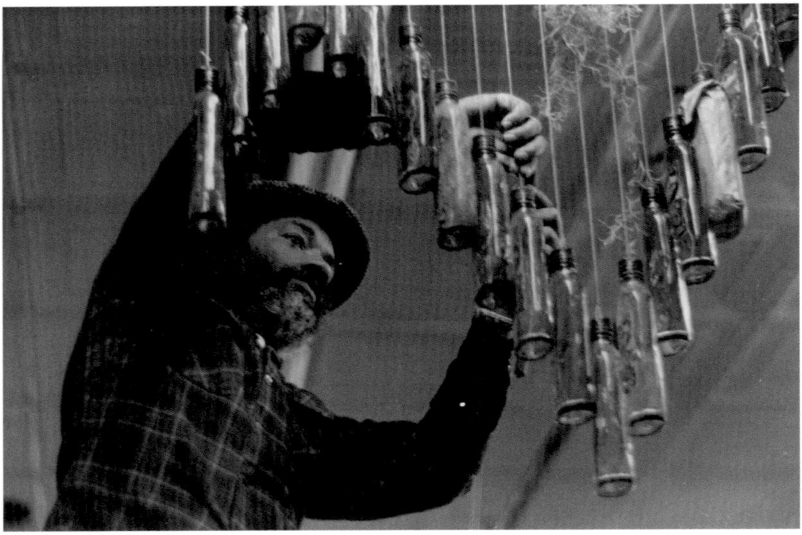

43. David Hammons creating a bottle
installation in his Harlem studio, c.1983
Photograph and courtesy Frank Stewart

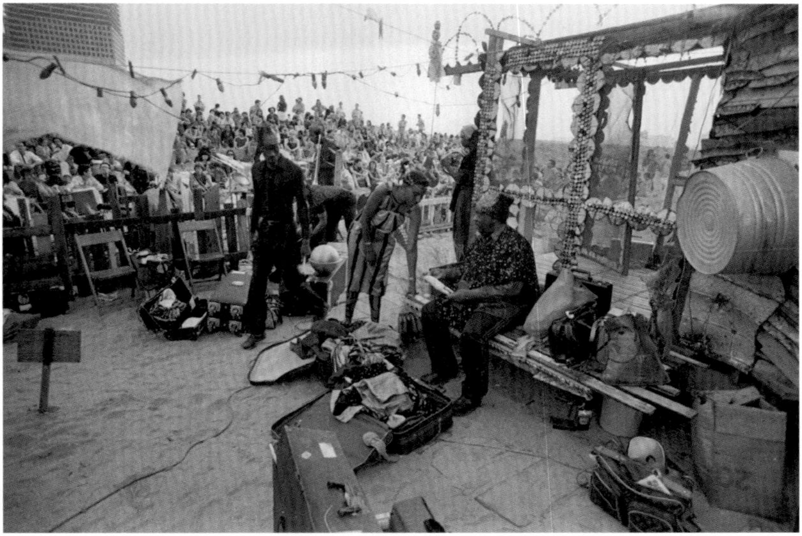

44. Sun Ra and his Arkestra preparing for their concert on David Hammons's *Delta Spirit* (also known as *Spirit House*), made with Angela Valeria and Jerry Barr, 1985, part of 'Art on the Beach', Battery Park in New York
Photograph and courtesy Frank Stewart

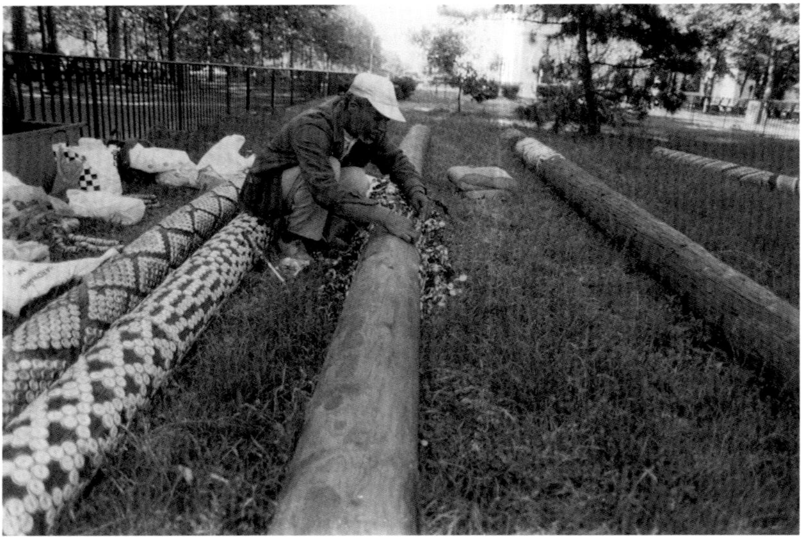

45. David Hammons making
Higher Goals for Cadman Plaza in
Brooklyn, 1986
Photograph: Dawoud Bey
Courtesy Exit Art Archives,
Fales Library and Special Collections,
New York University

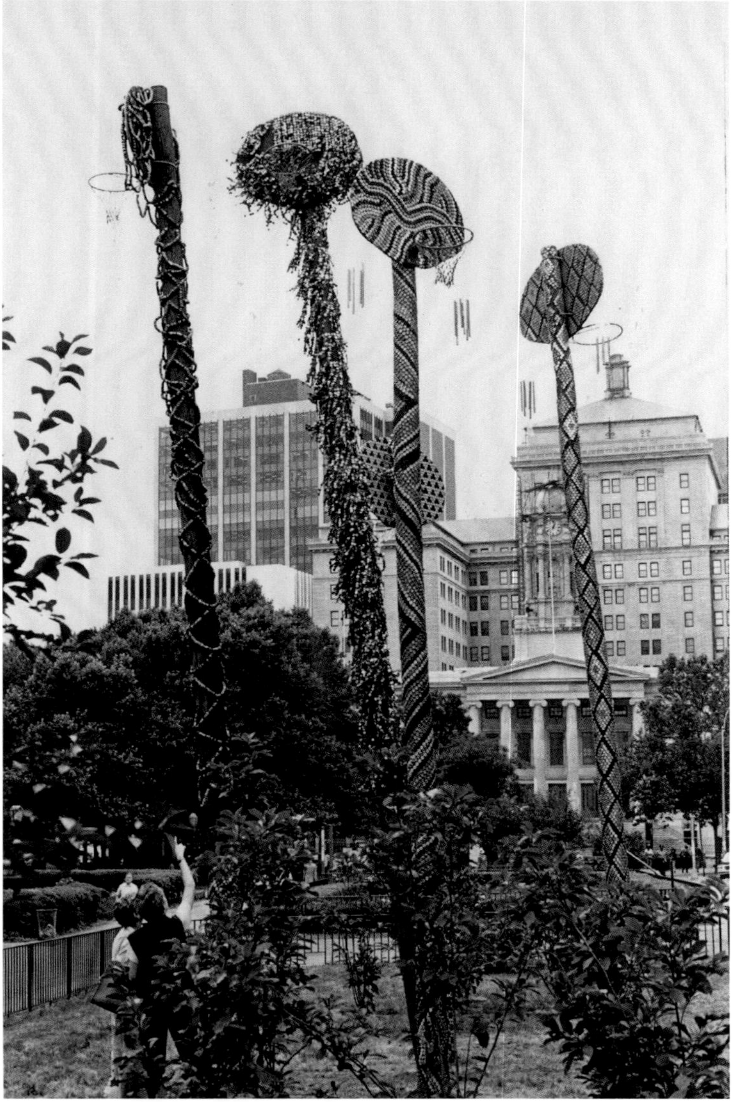

46. David Hammons,
Higher Goals, 1986,
Cadman Plaza, Brooklyn
Photograph: Pinkney Herbert /
Jennifer Secor
Courtesy Public Art Fund, New York

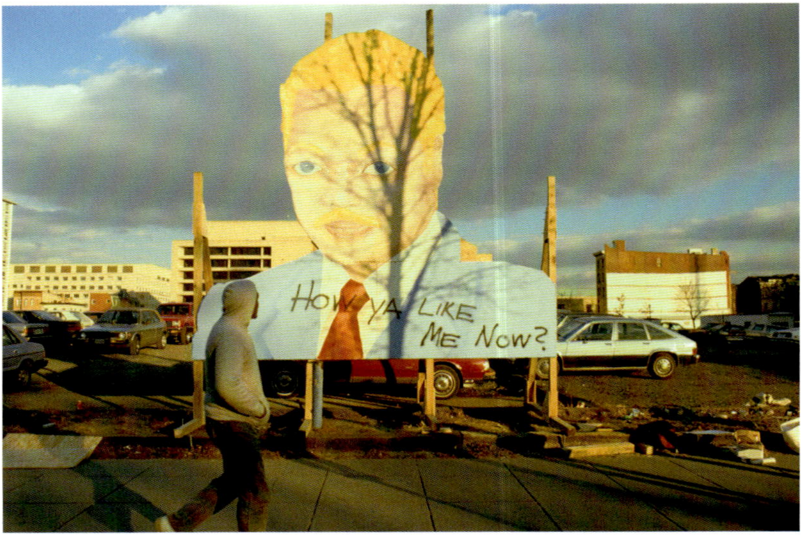

47. David Hammons,
How Ya Like Me Now?, 1988,
installed Washington DC, 1989
Photograph: Philip Brookman
Courtesy the Corcoran Gallery of Art,
Washington DC

> *uptight because the paper's so expensive, they're afraid to be loose on it when they already put the investment up. And they're like, 'I got to make a good piece of art!'* [laughs] *Ain't nothing gonna happen with that kind of consciousness.*[141]

Thus 'it was an easy move', Hammons remembers, to go from peddling snow to his next project: making sculptures out of elephant dung, starting in 1985.[142] He collected the excrement from Brooklyn's Prospect Park Zoo (predominantly from an elephant named Nancy, as he told critics) and anointed each lump with a bit of paint, toy-car wheels, peanuts, chains and other readymade bling. Unlike Piero Manzoni's safely preserved 1961 *Merde d'artiste* (*Artist's Shit*), Hammons removed the aura and 'authenticity' of a product 'made' by the artist, as well as the protection of the hermetically sealed can. Hammons's shit declares what it is without allowing any collector to get around its abject materiality. That streetwise alchemy so prevalent elsewhere in his work is here dazzlingly literalized: Hammons was making an art of turning shit into gold.

Yet, his is an ambivalent relationship to money. While Hammons critiqued artists who were making soulless things simply to buy bigger lofts, and he himself abandoned art forms as soon as they became too easy a source of revenue (for example, his body prints), he also announced, just a few years after *Bliz-aard Ball Sale*:

> *It's possible to sell pieces for $100,000 that are the size of my palm. 'Cause this is a cultural statement that they have to address. Buying a small piece for $100,000 from a black artist, who just took two, um, pipe cleaners and put them together, you know, 'cause I'm interested in making that cultural statement towards the art world.*[143]

Because the money that circulates within a predominantly white art world is inextricably bound to issues of class and race.[144] And in the case of *Bliz-aard Ball Sale,* Hammons might have known that his clients, the buyers of those things the size of his palm, would be, as Bey remembers, 'All white, by the way. White college-aged students. Ain't no black person gonna pay you for a snowball. [*laughs*] That's *not* gonna happen.'[145]

As Black as Their Art is White

I am an artist, but I am not on the side of the art world.
– David Hammons [146]

I realize I'm saying some things that you think can get me in trouble, but, brothers, I was born in, trouble.
– Malcolm X [147]

How to speak of the terrible reduction that is racism and the singular way Hammons addresses it – honouring the artist's complex and nimble understanding of blackness, his way of both celebrating it and troubling it, at once adopting racial slurs and literally running them over with his Volkswagen? For Hammons, his reasoning has been simple: 'I always had to see their [white] reflections when I looked at Western Art. There is no information in there concerning my reference points. So, my art had to be as Black as their art is white.'[148]

Evading perfection, sheen and system almost from the start, Hammons's artworks are often flimsy and funny, but also emphatically *loaded*. Materially, linguistically, spiritually and ideologically, they are a testament to the life that his materials had before he claimed to have found them, whether they be (invariably dirty) hair clippings throbbing with 'peoples' spirits' or wine bottles marked by 'a black person's lips [that] have touched each one'.[149] The result is a peculiar form of base materialism, dense with embedded information: ornery, mannered, anthropological and laced with what he has often called 'tragic magic'.[150] Finkelpearl deems the combination a veritable philosophy, recognizing in Hammons's 'ideology of dirt' a keen understanding of how spirit-laden materials can create 'a cultural representation, a picture of African-American culture'.[151]

Dirt, that oft-used material in Hammons's artistic repertoire, is, we cannot forget, 'matter out of place', as Mary Douglas theorized in 1966.[152] In other words, a contravention of class and taste that is, as the anthropologist explained, 'a by-product of systemic ordering and classification of matter'. Hammons makes clear to all that the nasty dirt he brings into the gallery or your home is not just any dirt, it is 'Harlem dirt' (or Springfield dirt, from his hometown), acting as 'matter out of place' when that 'place' is the lily-white art world. Because in the material there is the political. Accordingly,

Hammons admits that he first turned to black hair because it was 'the only thing then that was not of the oppressors' culture'.[153] As he has elsewhere acknowledged, 'Those pieces were all about making sure that the black viewer had a reflection of himself in the work', adding, 'white viewers have to look at someone else's culture in those pieces and see very little of themselves in it'.[154]

Dirty, acerbic, knowingly elegant, ferociously intelligent: Hammons's works are all of these things, even when they make you laugh out loud, or seem like an easy punchline. Because more often than not, the joke bites back. After all, has any single line inscribed on an artwork said more (in as few words) about aspirational culture, race relations and American politics than the tag *How Ya Like Me Now?* on a portrait of a blonde, white-faced Jesse Jackson? When Hammons drolly placed a lone pants zipper inside a bowl of granulated sugar and titled it *Fly in the Sugar Bowl* (1993), how could you not think of James Baldwin's 'Fly in the Buttermilk' (1958), a portrayal of the ravages of class, race and privilege felt by a black student at an all-white school (fig.57)?[155] When he took a Congolese wooden sculpture traditionally used to ward off evil spirits, painted the double-headed, nail-studded dog orange and titled it *Orange Is the New Black* (2014), he added, tongue-in-cheek, a reference to a then-current television series while revealing a painful truth about the incarceration of blacks in America, provoking us to ask: who needs protection from whom? Still, how could an empty cola bottle dangling from a blind man's cane, *Coke Cane* (1989, later renamed *Blind Reality*), or a set of old electric fans with their cords hanging listlessly on top of a large boulder at a traditionally white college, *Rock Fan* (1993), not just make you laugh?

His titles – playful, irreverent and never *necessarily* fixed – are 'all inside word games', he says, embedded with layers of meaning and inextricable from black cultural modes of signification.[156] Along these lines, Greg Tate writes: 'With Hammons, you often get as much fatalism as sly gallows humour, but because his works take their complex feelings about race, death and desire into the public square, they presume no transcendence or representation of black folk's circumstances that cannot be critiqued by the folk themselves.'[157] *Bliz-aard Ball Sale* was no exception to his linguistic interest. With its single *z*, dash and double *a* – like the colloquial drawing out of 'bad' into 'baaad', or Melvin Van Peebles's repeated letters in the title of his 1971 proto-blaxploitation film *Sweet Sweetback's Baadasssss Song* – Hammons makes a point of letting you know that no matter how seemingly simple the act, his sense of street vernacular and his poetic mode of 'signifyin'' is present.[158]

Joseph Beuys's fat and felt is often compared to Hammons's 'kinky' hair and barbecue bones, but Hammons isn't making art centred around a mystical narrative of the singular artist: his is no tale of being saved by Tatars in the mountains. Instead of an individual myth, Hammons deliberately references something larger than himself: a history of blackness, a history of race relations; which is to say, nothing less than a history of America itself, as told through the forms, symbols, materials and products of the African diaspora in the US. But there are certainly other parallels between the artists, because if Beuys crashed outside of the zone of Western rationality to be rescued by nomadic shamans and emerge as a shaman himself, Hammons, for his part, crashed the party of a white racist society, wrapping himself in garbage and rejecting mainstream values to emerge as a vodou priest of sorts. And we might imagine Hammons's claim on the African spiritual traditions he draws from as somehow more 'authentic', but we cannot forget that there is mythical construction there as well (note how he has emulated the Kongo practices he read about in Robert Farris Thompson's studies, and that he could do so because the scholar had translated Yoruba into English).[159] As Hammons has told it: 'I be into memory more than the avant-garde.' And by 'memory', he meant the history of the black experience, including the black body as a traded commodity – he pointed to the cotton pods in his hand as he spoke that line.[160] This (embodied) history marked black culture as a collective memory along with the fast food, cheap wine and dirt-poor resourcefulness that became part of 'free' black American life following slavery. 'You have to go back to what we were before you go forward to what we want to be', Hammons has declared, adding, 'I am here to remind us what the fuck we came from.'[161]

African American he is, and 'African-American' is an epithet that clings to his work. Accounts of Hammons's practice list his 'black' materials, suggesting that these convey the decisive racial critique of his work; but his work's politics arguably lie not only in what his materials are and what they symbolize, but in how they act, *what they do.* In making his hair pieces, for instance, Hammons got lice several times, chalking this up as a hazard of the job.[162] But try explaining to a collector or institution that 'their' art object will begin moulting at the slightest gust of air or with any movement of the piece itself; or worse, that it might have contained, and possibly still propagate, lice.[163] The same is true for Hammons's fried chicken pieces; these attracted insects and smelled of rancid oil long after he made them – 'and not any fancy fry or even KFC, but instead the smell of bullet-proof-glass-greasy-spoon fry', as A.C. Hudgins insists.[164] Similarly, there were his works made from smoked ribs (his so-called barbecue bones), which dripped rendered fat wherever they hung when the weather got hot (imagine the scene: a collector discovering liquefied animal grease oozing from the artwork as summer dinner guests arrive).[165] Maybe that's why he called one such work *Wall Piece*: it was as much about the wall it sullied as anything else. Trouble is what those works are.

At the 'Times Square Show', a now-legendary exhibition initiated by the artist-activist group Collaborative Projects, Inc. (Colab) in a derelict building near New York City's Times Square in 1980, Hammons showed up uninvited. After introducing himself to two of the organizers, he carefully smashed empty Night Train bottles collected from the neighbourhood and lined the exhibition venue's stairwells with their glittering shards.[166] When the organizers protested the trail of broken glass, he shrugged, suggesting they deal with it, and promptly left.[167] For his 1990 exhibition at Tilton Gallery, Hammons created *Whose Ice is Colder?*, which gallery staff had to attend to by mopping up melting ice blocks and dragging replacement blocks into the space every few days over the duration of the exhibition (fig.51).[168] The eventual buyer of that work (or of another, *Cold Shoulder*, made that same year and comprised of three ice blocks, this time with winter coats draped over them) would have to commit just as much effort to display the piece (fig.52). Over two decades later, in 2003, demonstrating his consistent insistence on a disruptive practice, Hammons created *Untitled (Kool Aid)*, an abstract watercolour pigmented with the eponymous drink powder and covered by a white, raw-silk veil. When it was shown as part of a group show at the Museum of Modern Art in New York, it bore a wall label informing the visitor that, per the artist's request, this work could be viewed 'by appointment only'. Once the effort of making an appointment had been undergone (with only a small number of viewings possible per week), the viewer was asked to enter the institution through its back entrance; from there a museum employee took them to the piece, donning white gloves (also at the request of the artist) to 'reveal' the artwork. The image then seen, it should be said, was made from the soft-drink powder associated with the 1978 mass suicide in which over nine hundred people blindly 'drank the Kool-Aid', following cult leader Jim Jones to their deaths. Here, commenting on art world conformity, Hammons simultaneously reminds us that more than what you (think you) see, the entire operation to get to the artwork *is*, arguably, also the artwork – an operation in which visibility is determined by his rules of engagement. In other words, to exhibit Hammons's art, to own it, and sometimes even just to see it, is to have to *work* for the privilege.

Somewhat differently but no less impudently, Hammons has regularly changed (sometimes several times) the composition, presentation, constituent elements and title of any number of his pieces once they left his studio, thus rejecting the fixity, stability and finality of the conventional work of art, not to mention entirely challenging its role as a product to be easily consumed. After all, how are you to know *which* of his multiple, protean versions is the correct or final 'artwork' when it has mutated so many times? Or what to call it (or, should you say, *them*)? And how can a collector or a museum – or even history – register and hold on to an artwork whose form, and very name, is shifting and uncertain? It seems almost too fitting (if not actually programmatic) that the representational contours in Hammons's body prints are themselves slowly fading (disintegrating, in fact, because the combination of cooking grease and chalk-stick pigment is hardly stable). Through and through, Hammons has made an art of resistance, disruption and obfuscation, sometimes literally so.

One last anecdote perhaps bespeaks Hammons's ultimate relationship to his materials and to history: if asked by a collector to repair an element of a work that has been broken or lost, Hammons has been known to further break or simply dispose of the original artwork, replacing it with a new version, so little is he preoccupied with the aura of originality and the value accrued by a piece in the process of its becoming 'historical'.[169] He is perhaps unsympathetic to anyone who can't or won't understand that objects live (and get broken as part of that life) and don't need to be restored to some ideal original state. Collectors who know of this habit – and realize the exchange value lost by suddenly having a vintage piece tossed and replaced – have stopped asking him to repair works. In *Bliz-aard Ball Sale*, too, Hammons resolutely ignored the market's (and history's) demand for auratic relics, for tangible, stable, collectible things. He knows that the artwork's fixedness – like the amiable accessibility of the artist who trades obsequious behaviour for money and fame – is expected, commonplace. Hammons is instead playing the game with rules of his own devising – practising what Fred Moten calls 'fugitivity' and claiming 'the victory of refusing to arrive'.[170]

You can sense that Hammons takes pleasure in the demands that his artworks make on those who choose to be in their presence or own them. For his is an art that inserts dirt or grease or bugs or confusion in order to clog 'the system'. It interferes with the machinery of the institution of art, all the better to make apparent how its cogs move and its gears engage. Because that machine, including its collectors, museums, curators and procedures of validation and value formation, was – and still is – a white machine. When Hammons rolled a basketball along a Harlem pavement or a Springfield road and bounced the dirty ball against museum walls (as he did, for example, for his 'David Hammons: Hometown' exhibition, fig.58), he showed that resistance to the (white) institution of art need not be explosive; it can be light as dust, comprised of the very particles of everyday existence that mar it from within. It was just a few small moves from bringing dirt into art institutions, and from shunning the art world's 'more is more' imperative, to making the street a place for art while selling something that no collector or museum could own.

If the reactions to Hammons's works at the time of their making are any indication, his approach has hardly been reassuring, no matter the skin colour of the viewer.[171] Thus, if Henri Matisse famously would have art act as a comfortable armchair for the bourgeoisie, Hammons has made his life's work his refusal to let anyone from any class, black or white, even sit down.

Like Dirt to a Snowball

Art is a lily-white profession, and to be a fly in the sugar bowl is very dangerous.

– David Hammons[172]

Race is not a topic of *Bliz-aard Ball Sale*. About that Hammons is emphatic.[173] If the artist's early works attempted quite vocally to reflect his experience, echoing his admission that 'all of the things that I see socially – the social conditions of racism – come out like a sweat', he also quickly realized that he did not want to 'get trapped into making cultural statements'.[174] As he pointed out in 1994:

> *I'm trying to get away with the redundancy of being an African American or making African-American art. It's like a double negative, a double noun. So I'm trying to figure it out. Everyone knows that I am black, so my work doesn't have to shout it out anymore. ... I am black. The work will automatically be thought of as a part of my African-American culture.*[175]

The blackness so mordantly commented on in his larger oeuvre is not *Bliz-aard Ball Sale*'s subject, no matter how black his skin or how white the snowballs, and no matter how much it might appear that through this action whiteness itself was being sold as a commodity. Instead, Hammons reminds us, it was humorous: an act with a touch as playful as the coloured mittens he wore while performing it. And to not recognize and respect that would be to turn the intention of the act into something it wasn't. But to not talk about the relationship of the black body to the economy, or its relationship to the streets of New York City in the 1980s, is to miss an underpinning to the work that – intentionally or not – affected how it was read.

Hammons made his satire of commodity exchange at a moment when the wealth and prosperity of the (overwhelmingly white) upper class was fueling an unprecedented expansion of the art market, particularly in New York City. His chosen site for the sale, on the Lower East Side, was a crucible for the transformation of the city as a whole and a case study of the relationship of art and gentrification. The area had been a working-class neighbourhood for more than a century and a half prior to the financial crisis that hit New York in the 1970s. The departure of the middle class to the suburbs, and with them their tax dollars, resulted in cuts to vital social services including trash pickup, as well as fire station closures and limited public transit service.[176] By the mid-1970s, landlords were walking away from their buildings, creating an epidemic of residential abandonment (they sometimes cut their losses with 'arson-for-profit' insurance schemes that left behind an urban landscape of burned-out tenement buildings).[177] In the wake of this, and well into the 80s, an underground economy of drug sales, especially heroin and crack cocaine, spread throughout Lower Manhattan, not far from where *Bliz-aard Ball Sale* took place. Sellers lowered baskets from apartment windows to their clients below, while bodegas and liquor stores also dealt. Theft became prevalent as desperate junkies sold their wares at improvised street markets alongside immigrants and other members of the urban poor.[178]

By the late 1970s, the cheap real estate had drawn artists and musicians to the area, giving shape to a 'downtown' scene. Located between the skyscrapers of Wall Street and Midtown, with SoHo to the west, the East Village was earmarked in the mid-80s by developers as the next lucrative locale, enhanced in no small part by its art scene. Real-estate speculation meant the displacement of long-term residents and eventually even of the artists themselves, whose presence and reputation played a key role in the neighbourhood's gentrification.[179]

Ronald Reagan, we should not forget, was president by 1981, and his administration's much publicized 'war on drugs' perfectly dovetailed with the pro-development agenda advanced by New York Mayor Edward Koch. The NYC police were running anti-loitering campaigns and periodically busting the ad hoc outdoor flea markets along St Mark's Place, Second Avenue and Avenue A, which newer residents and developers found to be eyesores and obstacles to their preferred image of the area. Reagan's 'trickle-down' economics reigned: tax cuts for the rich, decreased social spending, increased military spending and deregulation of domestic markets. It was an era characterized by junk bonds and leveraged buyouts, extraordinary excess and mottos like Gordon Gekko's 'greed is good'. It was an era of TV series devoted to the lives of the super rich, from *Dallas* to *Dynasty*, of so-called power dressing and shoulder pads – an era, in other words, in which having, making and spending money, or giving the impression of having the power that went with it, was consummately fashionable. Much of that capital found its way into an art world all too happy to get champagne-drunk on it. Between 1982–85, more than one hundred galleries opened in New York, almost all on the Lower East Side; gallery sales in the city approached one billion dollars in 1983 alone, the very year of *Bliz-aard Ball Sale*.[180] It was a time, as art critic Jerry Saltz famously put it, 'when art and money had sex in public'.[181]

Hammons's sales ventures, the snowball sale as much as his subsequent doll shoe sale, were thus laced with timely critique. As Robert Farris

Thompson observed about the latter sale, 'it was not a "happening". It was materially coded, material banter, a search for counter-wit.'[182] For instance, when Hammons corrected passers-by who made jokes about the impressive overabundance of tiny shoes for sale being like Imelda Marcos's collection (it's excessiveness was revealed in 1986, when her dictator husband was ousted from rule in the Philippines), he answered: 'No, they're Nancy Reagan's. You just haven't looked in her closet lately.'[183] The joke hurt. Rather than letting viewers believe that luxuriant excess in the face of widespread poverty existed only elsewhere, the artist pointed to problems closer to home.[184] As Greg Tate noted early on:

> *Those performances were about Hammons humbling himself as well, putting his stuff out on the streets with other hustlers and peddlers and dealing with their discriminating and derisive audience. In the marketplace of the street, Hammons puts to shame the art-world idea that an artist's conceits are more valuable and worthy of preservation than preserving a human life.*[185]

The woozily optimistic Saturnalia of the 80s masked a socially catastrophic flip side: unemployment, affecting twelve million Americans, was at its highest figure since 1941; accompanying it was widespread homelessness, violence and precariousness for the poor. In 1983, more than fifteen per cent of the US population lived below the poverty line, with dire consequences for working-class blacks.[186]

Urban space was, in the years surrounding Hammons's *Bliz-aard Ball Sale*, quite simply the primary place for the '"invisible men" of the late capitalist underclass', to borrow Kobena Mercer's words.[187] Often unable to get jobs in legitimate industries, these urban poor survived in shadow economies. The streets were where the jobless and desperate passed their time and sold trash-picked goods. *Bliz-aard Ball Sale* was thus not only a decidedly ephemeral counterproposal to the art world and material lust of the 80s. It must also be recognized in the context of an era when countless black men and women were pushed even further into the margins of society.[188] This was particularly evident on the street, where Hammons staged his sale.

Bliz-aard Ball Sale is not 'about' any of this. Yet the reality of America's collective racial imaginary clings to it, like dirt to a snowball. And that is the case even if we know that race is a construction rather than an immutable category belonging to some natural order; a construction, moreover, that Hammons consistently troubles. Snow itself acts as a semantic agent, linked to whiteness and purity ('pure as the driven snow', 'white as snow', 'Snow White', etc.). Think of the opening line of Frantz Fanon's 1952 essay 'The Fact of Blackness': the exclamation 'Look, a Negro!' prompts his analysis of race as a visual phenomenon, exploring how black identity is 'constructed' through the white gaze.[189] The sight of Hammons's sales offering in 1983 would have elicited a similar reaction – not only 'Look, a snowball!', but also 'Look, a black man selling a snowball!' In other words, the reactions of passers-by to a black salesman loitering on the pavement could not avoid being filtered through racial and historical entanglements lying outside of the work, no matter what Hammons says about it.

Perhaps one should see *Bliz-aard Ball Sale* all the more in relation to a work like *Pissed Off*, where the arrival of a policeman probably occurred as much because Hammons was caught in the act as because he was, statistically speaking, already a subject of suspicion as a black man wandering the streets in a predominantly white business and government district.[190] You cannot think of these works or of Hammons's street actions in general without reckoning with what blackness meant (and means still) in public space. Or without acknowledging that by putting himself out on a street corner with his wares, Hammons may well have been playing with racist stereotypes associated with blacks (homeless vagrant, street hustler, drug pusher) and at the same time undercutting them through his calm, serious stance and wilfully elegant style. The adage 'the white man's ice is colder' speaks for the sort of internalized racism that causes black Americans to believe that businesses, products and services offered by whites are better, more reliable.[191] Turning the expression on its head, Hammons's act implicitly suggested that although you could easily make your own snowball, this black man's ice was worthy of purchase; it was perhaps colder, even. Despite his claim that he did not consciously think of race when conceiving or performing *Bliz-aard Ball Sale* (and I do believe him), its viewers would have likely thought of it *for him*. 'Like misogyny', as Teju Cole put it in *The New Yorker*, racism 'is atmospheric. You don't see it at first. But understanding comes.'[192]

If some of Hammons's viewers have perpetuated racism as unthinkingly as breathing air, mainstream art history, for its part, has too. The very year of *Bliz-aard Ball Sale*, the critic and art historian Rosalind Krauss is reported to have told fellow attendees at a seminar sponsored by the National Endowment for the Arts that she 'doubts there is any unrecognized African-American art of quality because if it didn't bring itself to her attention it probably didn't exist'.[193] She clearly wasn't looking among the street sellers on the south-east corner of Cooper Square and Astor Place (or, for that matter, taking the 'funk lessons' Adrian Piper was offering that same year). And in light of that startlingly myopic statement by one of the period's preeminent art historians, one understands better why Hammons felt the need to place himself out on the street. As he once insisted: 'The art audience is the worst audience in the world. It's overly educated, it's conservative, it's out to criticize, not to understand and it never has any fun. Why should I spend my time playing to that audience? [...] So I refuse to deal with that audience and I'll play with the street audience.'[194]

Black Skin, White Cubes

I feel most coloured when I am thrown up against a sharp white background.
– Zora Neale Hurston[195]

An image comes to mind of a white, ideal space that, more than any single picture, may be the archetypal image of twentieth-century art; it clarifies itself through a process of historical inevitability usually attached to the art it contains. [...] *Never was a space, designed to accommodate the prejudices and enhance the self-image of the upper middle classes, so efficiently codified.*
– Brian O'Doherty[196]

Hammons has never been fond of white cubes. One thing you can say about *Bliz-aard Ball Sale* is that it showed to what lengths he would go to avoid them. Like Gustave Courbet's creation of a rogue pavilion just across the way from the official 1855 salon exposition in Paris, Hammons's carefully organized display of snowballs near the pristine white cubes of the burgeoning gallery scene was somewhere between a huckster's outdoor sales showroom and his own *salon des refusés*. However, if a kind of *salon des refusés* it was, then Hammons had arranged it without having tried and failed to penetrate any official salon. He had, from the start, refused to accept the art world's conventional procedures and tidy sensibilities (its rules and paths to career building), as well as the character and display logic of its spaces, once declaring:

> *Most of my things I can't exhibit because the situation isn't right. The reason for that is that no one is taking the shit seriously anymore. And the rooms are almost always wrong, too much plasterboard, too overlit, too shiny and too neat. Painting these rooms doesn't really help, that takes the sheen off but there's no spirit, they're still gallery spaces.*[197]

Part of his resistance to such spaces is based on who gathers in them and the nature of their attention: 'People aren't really looking at art, they're looking at each other and each other's clothes and each other's haircuts.'[198]

Bliz-aard Ball Sale's force lies not only in how seamlessly it blended into its urban context, but also in how diametrically opposed that context was to the conditions of the white cube with its inbuilt audience. And, just as early presentations of Hammons's work hung on pegboards or near to swimming pools paved the way for his various sales activities on the street, later endeavours further confirmed his enduring pursuit of unconventional sites to show his art. These often involved, like *Bliz-aard Ball Sale*, an interrogation of consumer exchange. A perfect but little-known example is his untitled, unannounced 1994 exhibition at Knobkerry, a shop selling African and Asian artefacts, where his objects slyly infiltrated the emporium's usual commodities with no indication of their distinct status (fig.60); or his 2004 contribution to Dak'Art, the biennial of contemporary African art in Dakar, Senegal, where he organized *Sheep Raffle*, a daily animal lottery for local residents at a busy crossroads, in order to give people who think biennials are for 'white people' instead 'something they can relate to' (fig.63).[199] These projects remind us that the whole of Hammons's life work to date has entailed, on the one hand, evading art institutions and their coolly antiseptic spaces and, on the other, revealing the power, race, class and fiduciary dynamics that inflect them.

In 1976, across a trilogy of essays published in *Artforum*, Brian O'Doherty made abundantly clear that the white cube was not a neutral site, calling it nothing less than 'a social, financial and intellectual snobbery which models (and at its worst parodies) our system of limited production, our modes of assigning value, our social habits at large'.[200] O'Doherty articulated this just as Hammons was showing up the white cube as an implicitly racialized space - its walls as white as the culture it tacitly upholds. As the artist would later say:

> *White walls are so difficult because everything is out of context. They don't give me any information. It's not the way my culture perceives the world. We would never build a shape like that or rooms that way. To us that's for mad people, you get put in them in the hospital. There is no other place I'd seen that kind of room until I came into the art world.*[201]

Hammons has often created disruptions literally aimed at this architecture. Whether he defiles its walls with fried food or lice-infested hair; covers them with the cheap, stencilled patterns of Harlem tenement hallways, or imprints them with dirt from a basketball (fig.58); has guests at the opening of his first museum survey play a pick-up game of basketball within the exhibition; empties the gallery of all signs of art and recasts the walls with blue light (fig.61); or quite simply leaves the walled-in institutionalized space altogether to present his art on the street or in a shop or at a dirt-covered crossroads, Hammons refuses to let reign unchecked the white cube and the 'prejudices' and 'self-image' of the society it is 'designed to accommodate'.[202] Zora Neale Hurston declared that she felt 'most coloured' when 'thrown up against a sharp white background'. Hammons has treated the white cube and the conventional models of exhibition that feature within it as that 'sharp white background', against which he would make a life work of responding.[203]

Colour Theory

There is a white fantasy which posits whiteness as the norm.
- Manthia Diawara[204]

A generation of artists in the 1970s and 80s were hailed for their critical enquiry into the workings of institutions that display, market and distribute art: critics and scholars called these types of strategies 'institutional critique'. They didn't ever use that term for Hammons's work, maybe because his actions were leavened by a grit and humour that dared to show its colour. Or maybe it was like the mordant ingenuity of his linguistic games and doublespeak, which, as Dawoud Bey tells us, 'was completely overlooked in the mainstream art press, thus proving one of the subversive tenets of signifying: it's hard to get the joke if the joke is on you'.[205] Whether the mainstream art world got his 'joke' or not, Hammons's practice has critically revealed the mechanisms of the art world itself, including dismantling the neutrality of the white cube and pointing to its inextricability from societal racism.

If Hammons translates what it means to be black in America, he does so while making work that uncovers the ways in which race is a concept formed by and tethered to a larger national, art-historical and Western imaginary. For his is only partly a portrait of black culture. It is as much a portrait of how that culture is read in a racist society. To understand Hammons's work, one must acknowledge and question the narratives of art history, which systematically posit whiteness as both neutral and as *the* universal position (what Diawara calls the 'norm'), while the black position is one of exception and difference. Hammons himself sees this tendency as commonplace, as he made clear in an exchange with an interviewer who began with the statement 'you did racial art in the 80s and 90s'. Hammons interrupted him: 'Wait. We are all involved in racial art. Andy Warhol was a racial artist. He talked about the art world through a white person's perspective, but when a black person does it, it's racial art.'[206]

Writing in 1994, a reviewer of Hammons's exhibition at the Illinois State Museum in Springfield made a point that seems not to have gained traction in the literature on the artist, despite of the acuteness of its observation:

> *Despite David Hammons's recent but hard-earned success – or perhaps because of it – you seldom hear his work described as intelligent or profound. 'Street-smart' maybe, but that's a term used to degrade a certain kind of intelligence or to embellish someone's otherwise white-collar acumen. And where the work of Mike Kelley or Martin Kippenberger is purported to tell profundities about the absurdity of human endeavour or the severity of our collective trauma, the wisdom in Hammons's work is*

rarely applied to any context outside his own African-American community. This is because Hammons is seen to be more accurate than intelligent – a kind of purveyor of the black experience – and hence many people in the art world appreciate his work, even respect it, but don't really think it has anything to do with them.[207]

To peruse art history is to see that few assessments of Hammons's work apply the same sorts of accolades to him as to his white contemporaries. Indeed, rarely is his work called 'intelligent'. And rarely, too, are his works referred to as 'vernacular' or 'popular' or reflective of 'American' culture without a hyphen or qualifier. This is what Toni Morrison, studying the white literary imagination, lamented when she observed that to be 'American' is to be assumed to be white (and male).[208]

Take as an example of this blind spot the critical reception of Mike Kelley, who, like Hammons, came of age in the Midwest and eventually studied art in Los Angeles, and who similarly and almost simultaneously turned to urban detritus and 'popular culture' (think of Kelley's use of knitted blankets, stuffed animals and pitiful, dirty ciphers of 'America'). His work is read as a statement about tropes of adolescence, the vernacular and low culture without 'white' ever being mentioned at all (never *white* adolescence, *white* vernacular or *white* low culture). Kelley's works – impertinent, tragic and loaded as they are, and sharing perhaps more with Hammons's concerns than art historians have admitted – are discussed as if they universally reflect popular culture *writ large*, and indeed Americanness *writ large*, while Hammons's works are spoken about almost uniquely in relation to black African-American culture.

Art at the opposite end of the spectrum from Hammons's could be equally cited. Jeff Koons first showed his immaculately ordered, Plexiglas-encased vacuum cleaners in 1980 in 'The New', which was part of a series of exhibitions involving a storefront-window at the New Museum in New York. The project that immediately followed that same year in the window was Hammons's *Rented Earth*, an exhibition set behind the same glass façade, this time X-ed out with masking tape; within, Hammons built walls meant to look shoddily plastered, and set mud, broken Thunderbird wine bottles, an African tribal mask and ritual staffs against a toy TV, platform shoes and piles of discarded pages from *The New York Times*. One critic

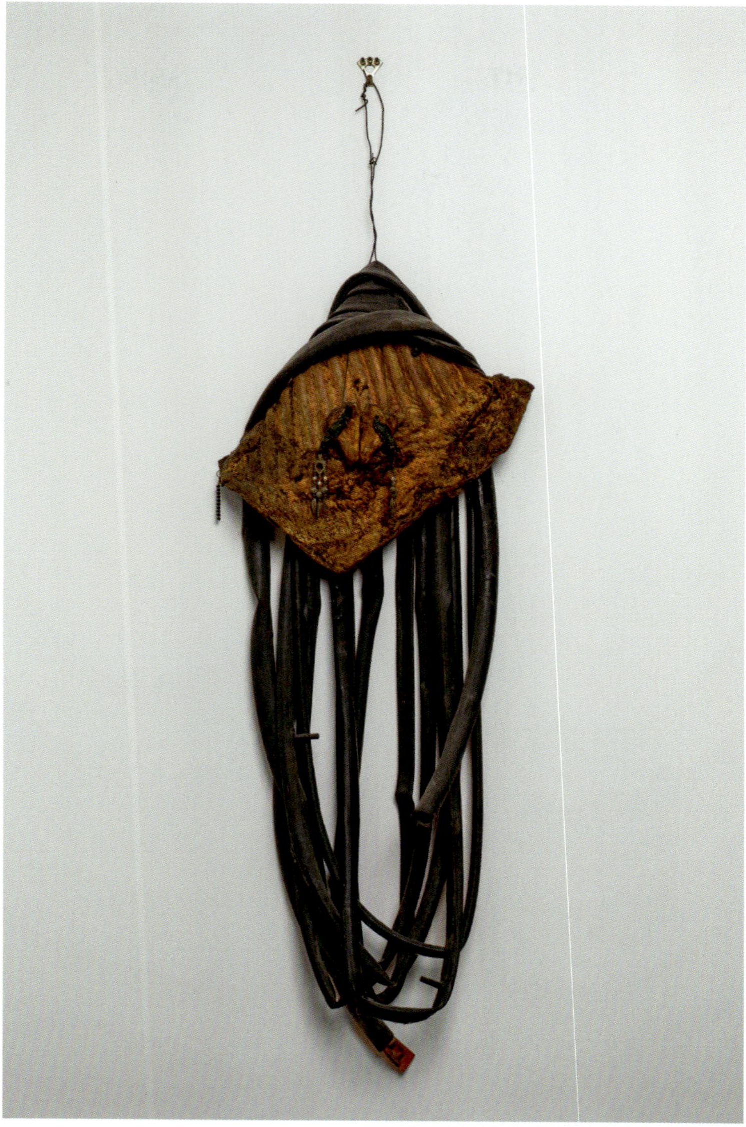

48. David Hammons,
Wall Piece, 1989,
ribs, chicken pieces, tyre inner tubes,
costume jewellery, gold leaf, paper, wire,
142.2 × 40.6 × 15.2cm

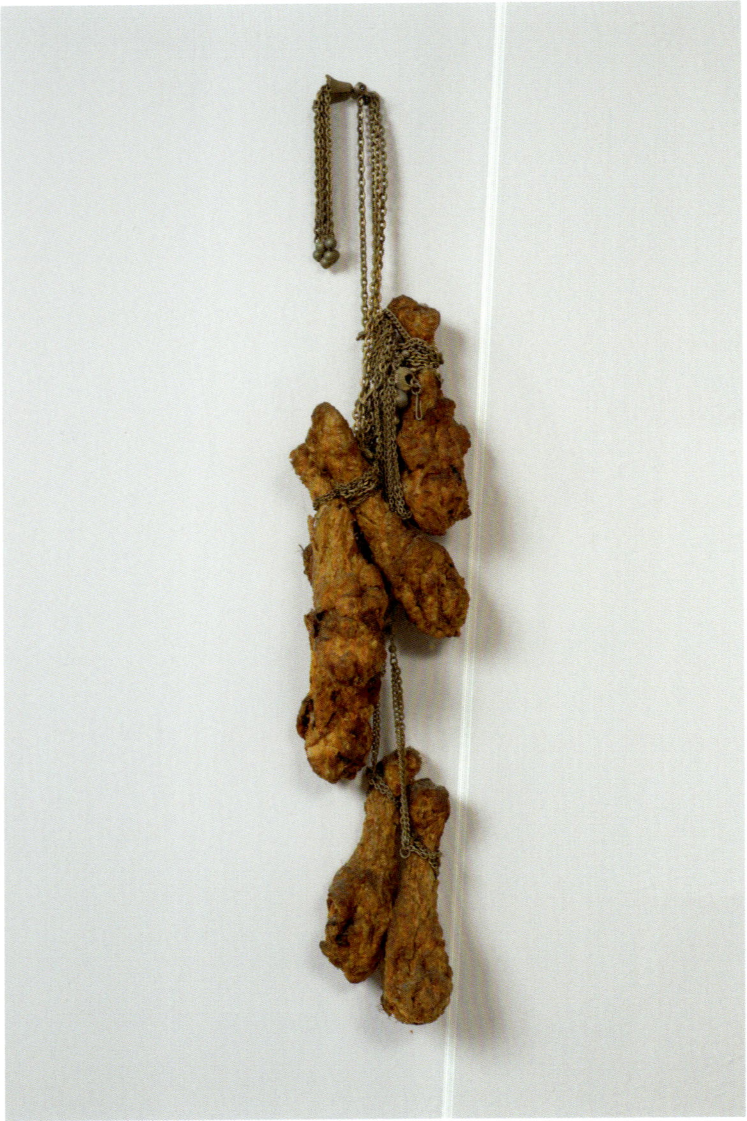

49. David Hammons,
Untitled (Fried Chicken Drumsticks and Chains), 1990,
fried chicken, metal costume jewellery,
48.2 × 11.4 × 8.8cm

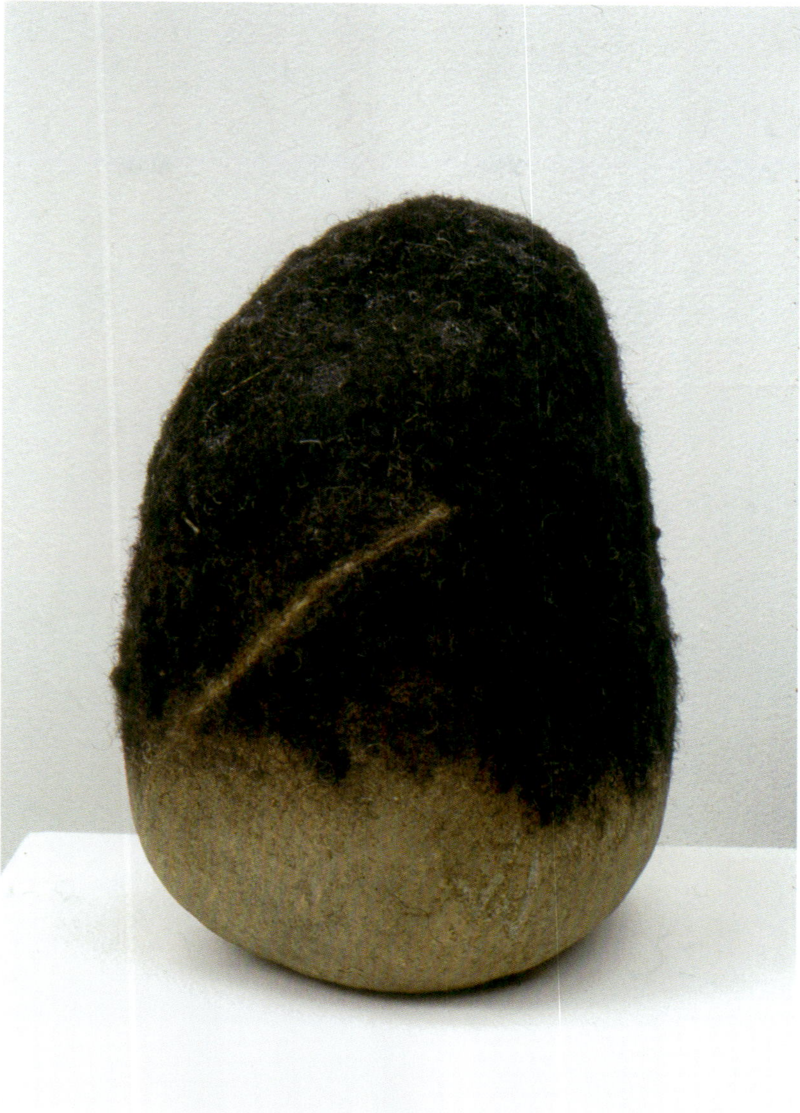

50. David Hammons,
Untitled (Rock Head), 1990,
rock, hair
Courtesy Tilton Gallery, New York

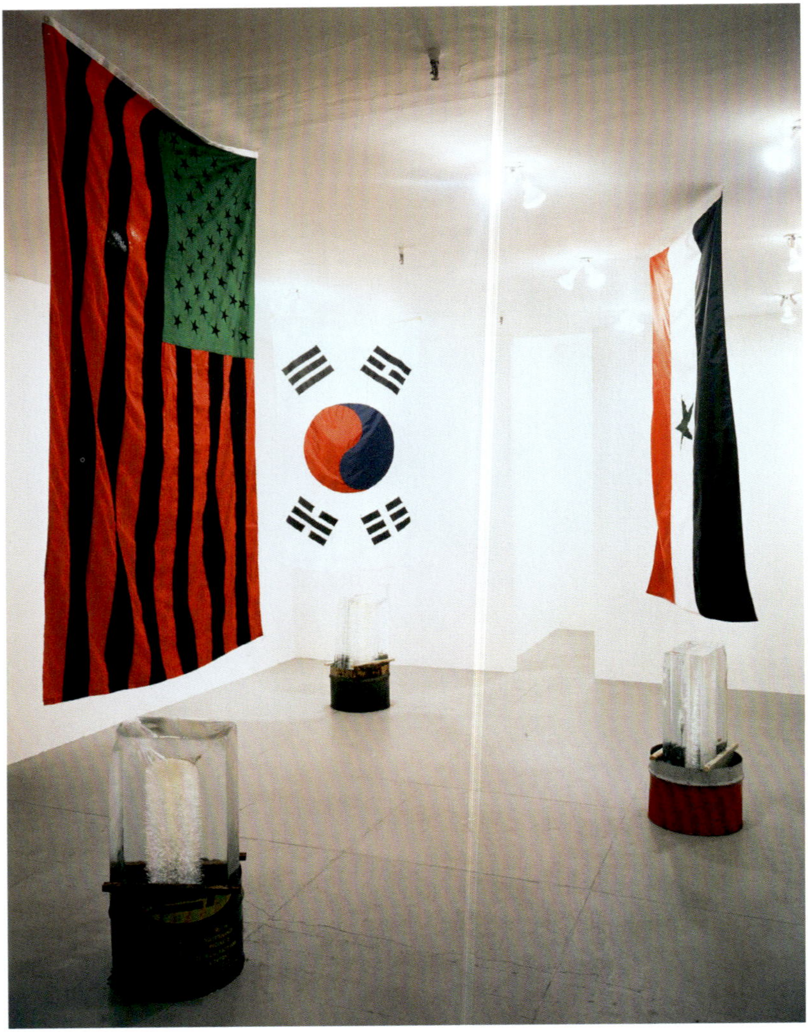

51. Installation view,
David Hammons,
Whose Ice Is Colder?, 1990,
Untitled (African-American Flag), 1990
(left), Korean flag, Yemenite flag,
ice blocks, oil barrels,
dimensions variable
Courtesy Tilton Gallery, New York

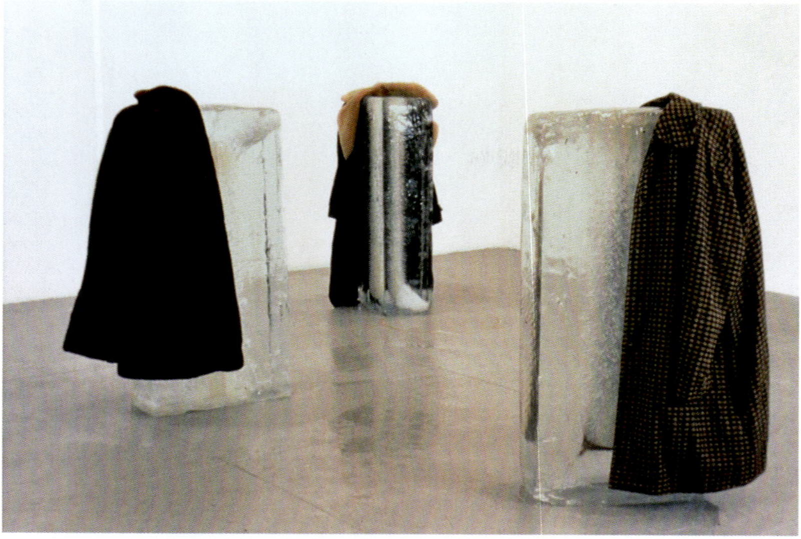

52. David Hammons,
Cold Shoulder, 1990,
ice blocks, jackets,
dimensions variable
Courtesy Tilton Gallery, New York

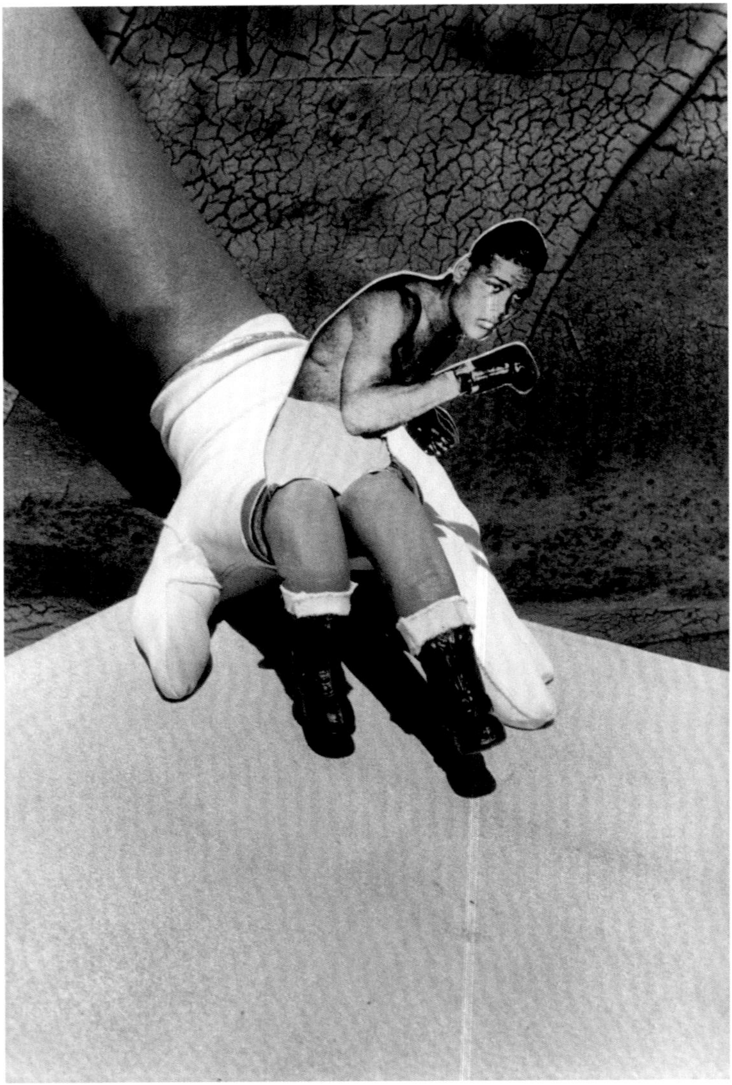

53. David Hammons,
St. Louis, 1990
Photograph: Dawoud Bey
Courtesy Exit Art Archives,
Fales Library and Special Collections,
New York University

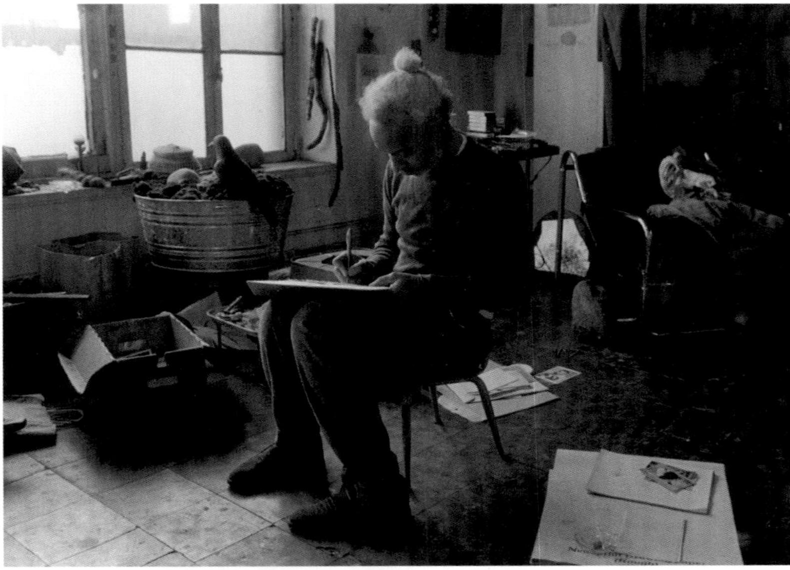

54. David Hammons in his studio,
125th Street, Harlem, c.1991
Photograph and courtesy Frank Stewart

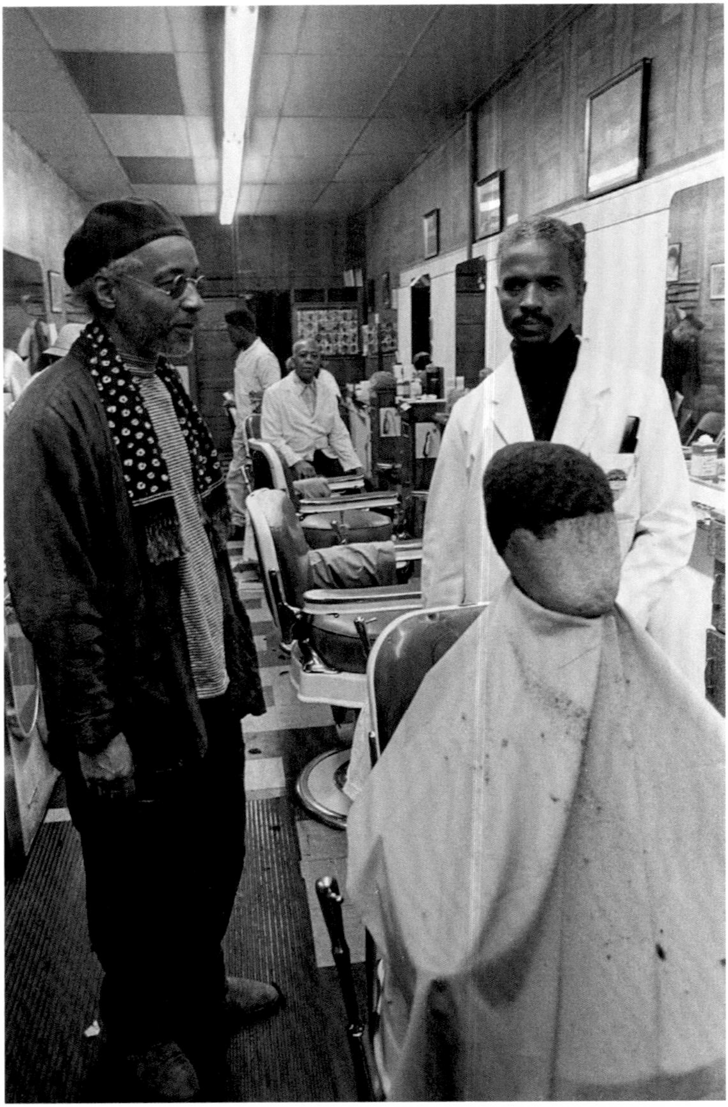

55. Performance view,
David Hammons, *Haircut*, 1992, Harlem
(with the artist and a barber)
Photograph and courtesy Coreen Simpson

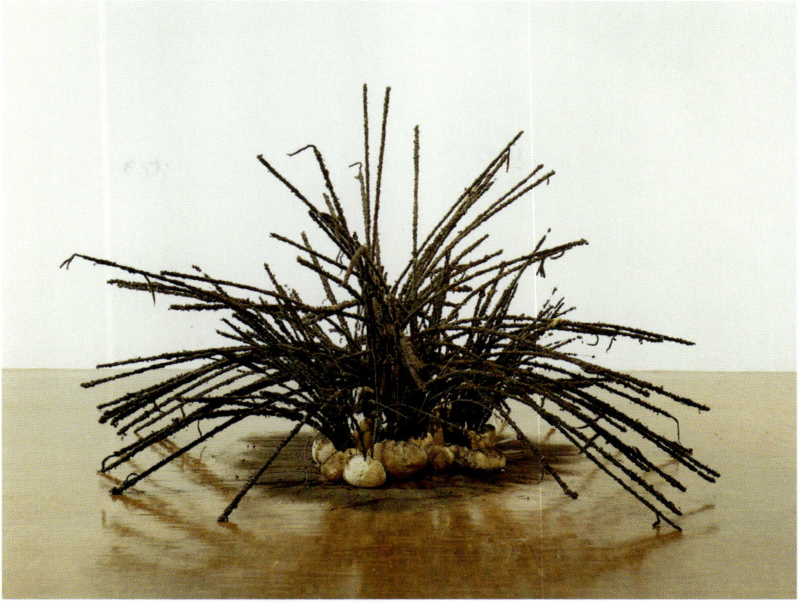

56. David Hammons,
Untitled, 1992,
human hair, wire, metallic mylar, sledge hammer, plastic beads, string, metal food tin, pantyhose, leather, tea bags, feathers, dimensions variable
Photograph: Geoffrey Clements

Courtesy Whitney Museum of American Art, New York; purchase, with funds from the Mrs Percy Uris Bequest and the Painting and Sculpture Committee 92.128a-z

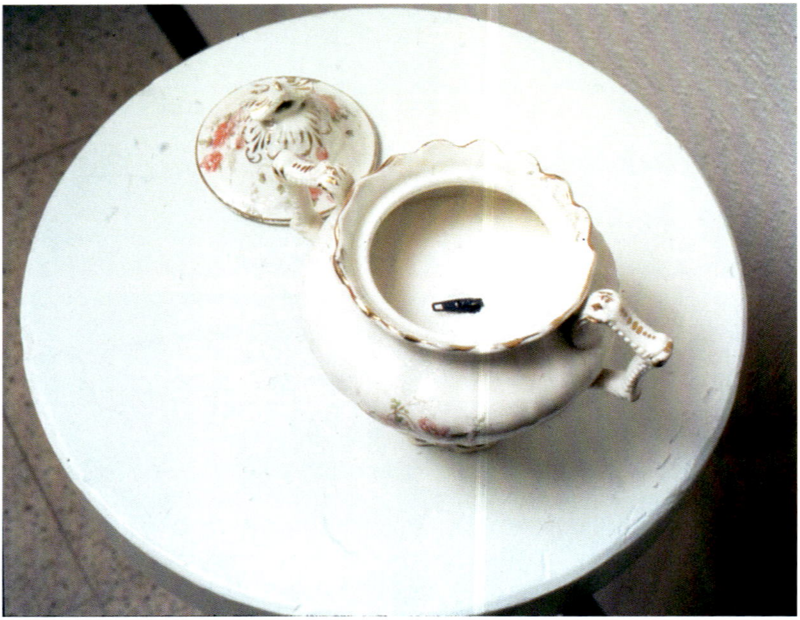

57. David Hammons,
Fly in the Sugar Bowl, 1993,
ceramic bowl, sugar, zipper fly
Courtesy Tilton Gallery, New York

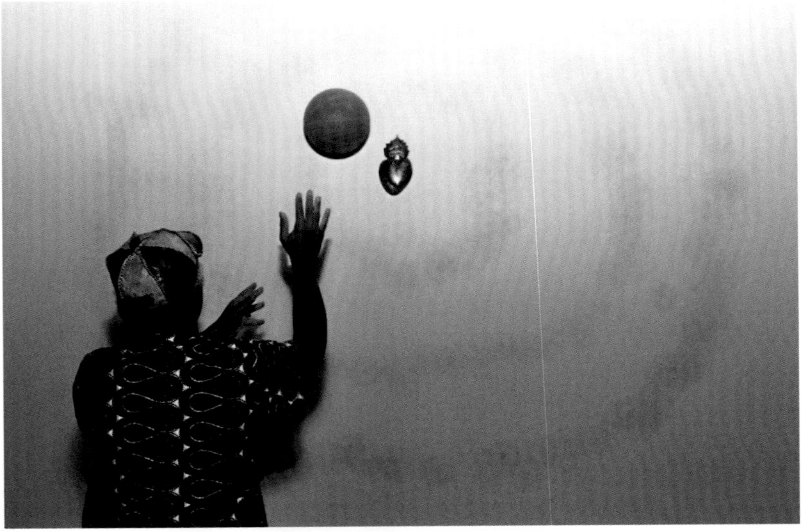

58. David Hammons creating
Untitled (Basketball Drawing), 1993,
for 'David Hammons: Hometown',
Illinois State Museum, Springfield, 1993
Photograph: Michael Tropea
Courtesy Illinois State Museum

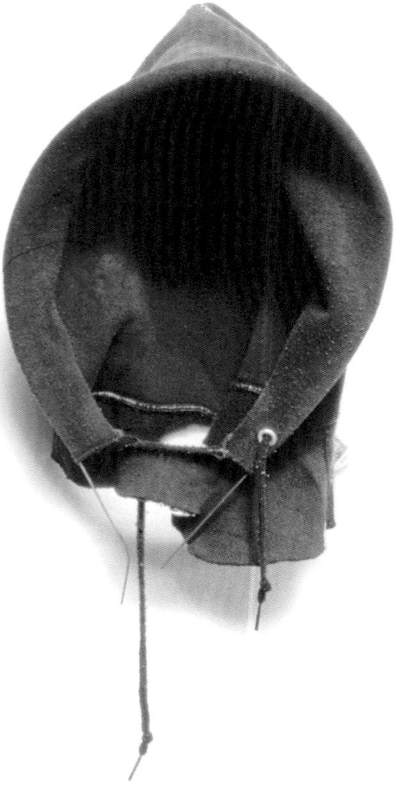

59. David Hammons,
In the Hood, 1993,
athletic sweatshirt hood with wire,
58.4 × 25.4 × 12.7cm
Courtesy Tilton Gallery, New York

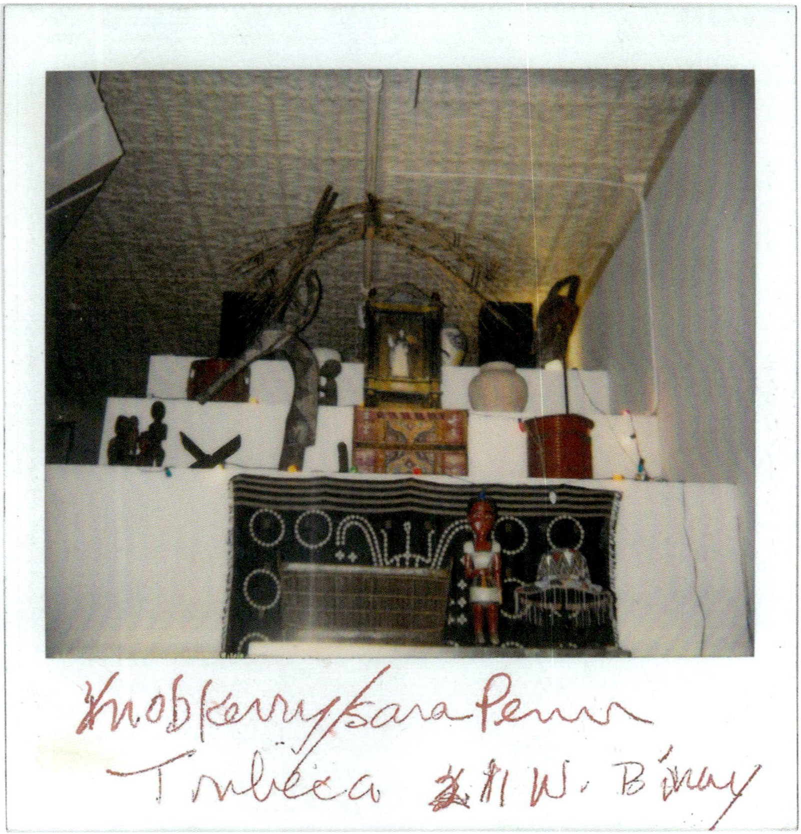

60. Installation view,
untitled exhibition, with *Flight Fantasy*,
1978, set among the store's regular
offerings, Knobkerry, New York, 1994
Photograph and courtesy Sara Penn

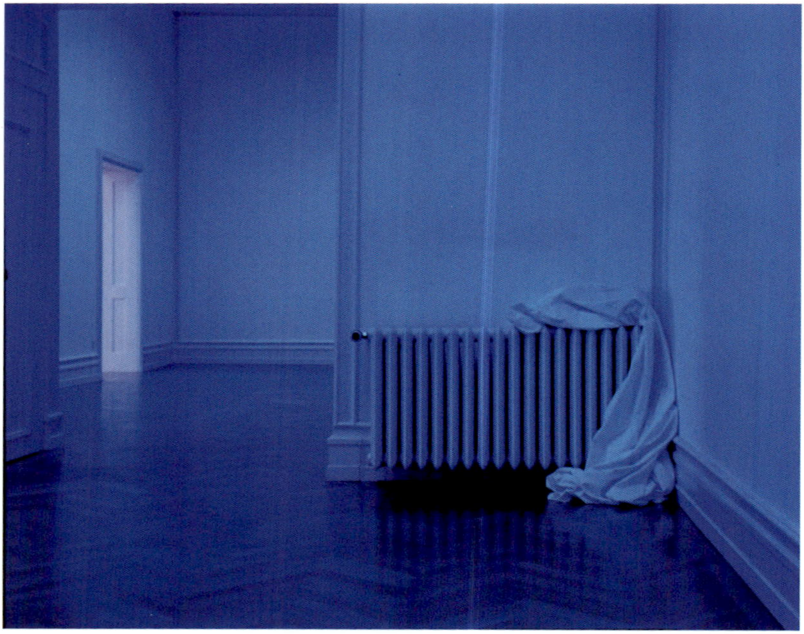

61. Installation view,
'David Hammons: Blues and the
Abstract Truth', Kunsthalle Bern, 1997
Photograph: Marco Schibig
Courtesy Kunsthalle Bern

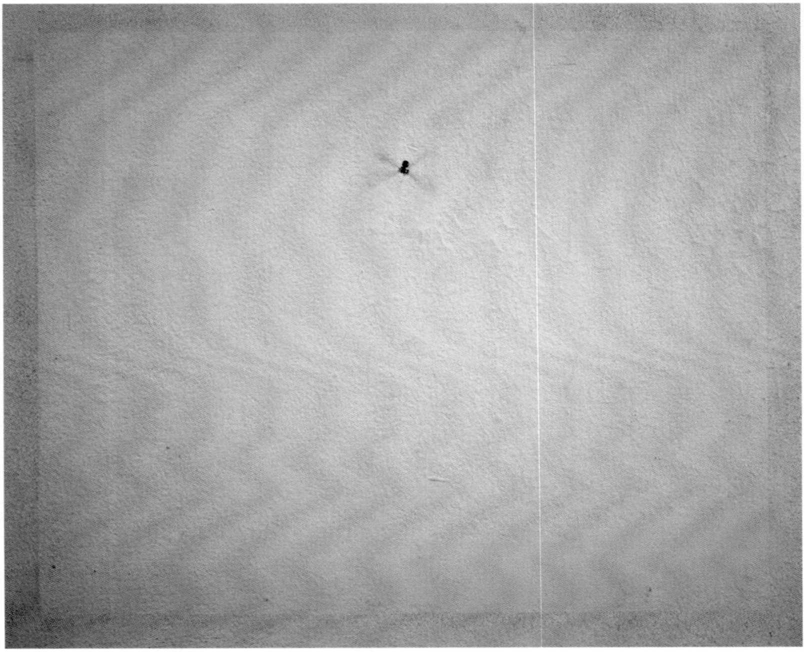

62. David Hammons,
Untitled (Dust Drawing), c.2001,
wall, dust, nail
Photograph and courtesy Erma Estwick

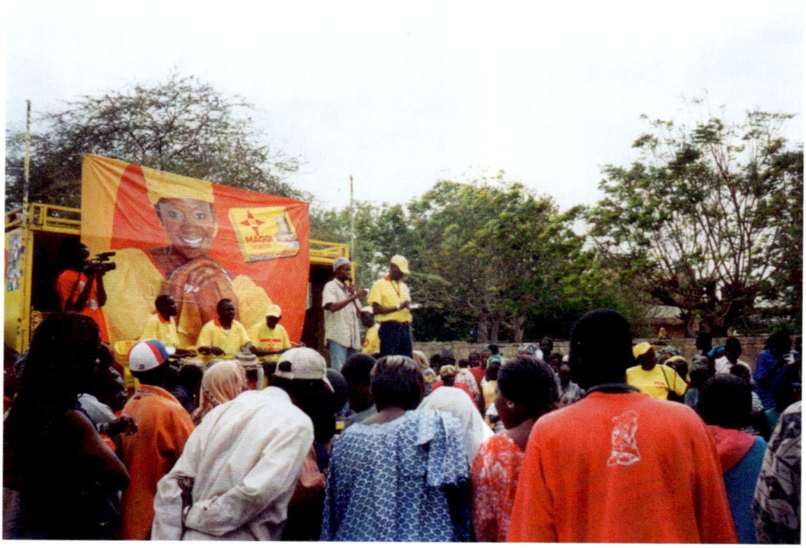

63. Performance view,
David Hammons, *Sheep Raffle*, 2004,
in 'Dak'Art: The Biennial of Contemporary
African Art', Dakar, Senegal, 2004
Photograph and courtesy Iolanda Pensa

declared Hammons's detritus 'shrapnel from the war between American and African cultures', noting that 'the mask and the staffs are so accomplished, so permanent, so beautiful; the American products so worn, so easily disposable'.[209] To have seen the projects back to back would have been to witness Hammons's recourse to dirt and African symbolism as a grungy, dark retort to Koons's decidedly white, middle-class, consumer branded 'American' symbolism. But no one mentioned the implicit 'whiteness' of Koons's project in their reviews, nor is it regularly spoken of in relation to his work to this day. In contrast, no reviewer failed to mention Hammons's 'blackness' then, nor have they since.

Part of the force of Hammons's works is the way in which they invoke black culture, all the better to make everyone, whatever the hue of their skin, see the larger context of an America grappling (still) with constructions of race. After all, *Fly in the Sugarbowl* is poignant, and bracingly revelatory, because it says as much about the 'fly' as it does about the sugar and the bowl. Or take Hammons's display of a slashed hoodie, *In the Hood* (1993), that is as much a commentary about black youth as about the white imaginary that allows racism to get lodged between homonyms: registering a hood as a hood from the hood (fig.59). The issue is not that Hammons's works are typically described in relation to the blackness that he deliberately invokes, but rather that too little is said about the whiteness that is implied as its foil.

Ice and Dust and Rumours

At the bottom of every rumour lies a secret. Otherwise they wouldn't be rumours, they'd be facts, wouldn't they?
– unusual artist[210]

What is an artwork that melts before your eyes? And what constitutes *Bliz-aard Ball Sale*'s work-of-art-ness anyway? Photographs may remain, but *Bliz-aard Ball Sale* truly exists, you could say, as hearsay, its details fugitive. Hammons situates the work of art in the vortex of a rethinking of the art object, precisely by making it disappear. But in case you might still consider its evasiveness a coincidental detail, rather than a willed aesthetic gesture that would declare itself to *be* the artwork, you need only look elsewhere in Hammons's practice to see that stealth and feints are recurrent. Not only does he refuse to be present and visible in the ways the art world typically expects of an artist, but the 'materials' that have come to constitute his artworks in the decades after *Bliz-aard Ball Sale* are similarly evanescent cousins of ice – from dust to even rumour itself.

In 2002, while visiting a Gerhard Richter retrospective at the Museum of Modern Art in New York with the poet Steve Cannon, Hammons is said to have had the idea to create an exhibition at A Gathering of the Tribes, the East Village cultural space run by Cannon. After learning that there was an exhibition of abstract paintings then on view at Tribes, Hammons came by the next day and proceeded to rub dust from the floor (or coal or newspaper – stories differ) around the framed edges of the paintings; he then removed them (temporarily exiling them to storage), leaving behind only the faintest trace of dust as an index of the paintings' previous presence on the walls.[211] The spontaneous 'exhibition' was unannounced and its duration unclear (perhaps only for a day), but it is said that the gallerist Jack Tilton came by with Robert Storr, curator of the Richter exhibition, having heard that there was a David Hammons exhibition on view. They didn't see any art upon entering, couldn't find the 'exhibition' and apparently left exasperated.[212]

This project connects to a series of so-called dust drawings that Hammons has created for friends and, in at least one case, a paying collector, using the dirt and dust found in their homes (or, for one sold at auction, at the auction house – site-specific these works were meant to be). He rubs the dust onto the wall around an existing framed artwork (or a paper template cut to the size of the artwork).[213] Leaving the telltale nail or wall hook on which the previous artwork had hung, with the faintest geometric trace of dust around it, Hammons's process makes art from nearly nothing (materially speaking) to put on view exactly the grime that comes from or belongs to a home (fig.62). If for years Hammons had made an art of bringing Harlem grease and dirt into homes and institutions to force viewers and collectors to confront where the artist 'was from', here he forced them to confront the filth that was their own.

Flitting, nearly indiscernible and yet pesky, dust might be the most fitting material counterpart to the evanescence of snow or the airy incertitude of rumour. In 2006, after having refused to participate in the Whitney Biennial on numerous occasions (his refusals having become a point of pride), Hammons finally conceded, but with the caveat of a set of strict conditions. These included, as recounted by one of the biennial's curators, that he would select from his own collection a work by Miles Davis, to be

> *shown in the middle of the exhibition, treated the same way as any other artwork – no special room for it, no special lighting. Second, the name of the lender was not to be disclosed, and the label would simply say that the painting was on loan from an anonymous collection. Third, the fact that Hammons was lending the painting to the Biennial, and therefore was taking part in the 2006 Whitney Biennial, was not to be revealed.*[214]

It was thusly that Davis's canvas *RU Legal*, from 1991, was included in the biennial and rumoured to be a gesture by Hammons – which the curators claim they dutifully refused to confirm. Effectively, Hammons orchestrated the inclusion of Davis in the biennial and the precise conditions of display, and he masterminded the conditions of communication concerning the work, since hardly a review or article about the exhibition failed to mention Hammons's alleged but unverifiable contribution.

A year later, his unofficial contribution to Skulptur Projekte Münster 07 was even more immaterial. He is said to have offered a prediction, a weather forecast (or 'a rumoured rumour', as Anthony Huberman rightly described it): word circulated that there would be rain on 18 August 2007, but it was nowhere officially announced.[215] Visitors wondered if his prediction, which is to say his 'art', would materialize. On the day in question, the sun shone and no rain came, but it was an artwork anyway. And Hammons pretty much got everyone who visited the outdoor exhibition to talk about the weather.[216] The following year, when invited to contribute to the 2008 Nuit Blanche in Paris, he forecast that a double rainbow would appear over the city on 4 October – again requesting an embargo on communication around the nature of his proposed artwork. Hammons claims that the organizers agreed, but then, a few days before the inauguration of the city-wide event, his name was removed from the exhibition roster and his 'project' cancelled. As he explained, 'I think they cancelled it because they couldn't explain it to anyone. But how do you stop or remove a rainbow from happening?'[217] And by the same token, how can you be sure that the 'artwork' wasn't precisely the tale that his prediction was accepted and then rejected, since the (new) rumour circulates anyway? As soon as an artist proposes to make an artwork that is a rumour, how can anyone stop or remove *it* from happening?

Sometime between the 'dust' exhibition at Tribes and the Münster prediction – I forget exactly when – it got around that Hammons had created a performance for an edition of the Venice Biennale: he commissioned an African street vendor to sell designer handbags, laid out on a rug and infiltrating Venice's illicit street commerce much as the snowballs of *Bliz-aard Ball Sale* had once done in New York City.[218] However, instead of fake Louis Vuitton, Gucci and Prada designs, Hammons's versions – it was said – were real, but would have been largely undetectable given how ubiquitous such street selling of counterfeits by African vendors is. Hiding in plain sight, the installation seemed perfectly plausible. Except, Hammons didn't actually stage it. Instead, the rumour probably emanated from a one-day performance by Fred Wilson, who, when representing the US in Venice in 2003, had organized for a vendor to sell unique handbags outside the US pavilion.[219] Hammons may well traffic in rumours, and a circulating rumour may have associated him with the act, but that doesn't mean it was a rumour *by* David Hammons – and it doesn't mean that it wasn't.

Little could be more furtive – and unreliable – than whispered information and hearsay. Otherwise 'they'd be facts, wouldn't they?', as the 'unusual artist' of John Farris's one-act play proclaims.[220] Rumours, like ice, like dust, are barely there; hardly visible or verifiable. They stonewall certitude and escape capture. Like Hammons himself, they constantly threaten to leave the room.

The Last Snowball

Bliz-aard Ball Sale has had several lives. The first was Hammons's act of selling the snowballs on that wintry day in 1983. The sale's most immediate aftermath was born of the circulation of its photographic record and the act's quasi-mythic presence over the years that followed. But before that afterlife could take hold – before, that is, the photographs actually circulated and the rumours gained their now-legendary proportions – Hammons organized the reappearance of a snowball from *Bliz-aard Ball Sale* three years following the original event. Or, you could say, he organized a particular afterlife that would help ensure his action's potential future and more enduring legacy. In 1986, at JAM's 503 Broadway location, the artist staged what was touted in the press release as Hammons's 'first solo exhibition in ten years'. Without any concrete information about what was to be presented, the typescript document bore the title 'Icestallation' with the date '2/13/83' printed just below. It was a cryptic declaration of sorts for those (almost everyone) who would have had no idea of the significance of the date; it acted like a purloined letter, under the noses of its readers but difficult to recognize as such.

The invitation cards printed for the occasion showed on one side JAM's practical information, including the 24 April–22 May 1986 exhibition dates, as well as the time and date of the opening reception and regular viewing hours. On the other side, which had been printed a solid silver-grey, Hammons individually hand-stamped the cards with a shimmering single 'ball' form. Being handmade, each print was a slightly distinct, imperfect impression roughly the size of a tennis ball (or a medium-sized snowball, if you will). They were, in fact, probably made from tennis balls, silver painted and then pressed onto the cards (as Hammons had once pressed himself onto paper for his body prints) (fig.69). At the bottom-right-hand corner, without a word of explanation, the cards each had the hand-written date '3/13/83', a full month off from the date on the press release. Some are scripted in Hammons's hand and others in Linda Goode Bryant's, who remembers the artist instructing her to finish adding the dates after his start. Goode Bryant doesn't recall specifically asking about the date, nor having noticed the difference between '2/13/83' and '3/13/83'. If both were meant to refer to the original 1983 snowball sale, and only one is actually correct, the press release is probably the more dependable source, pointing to that thirteenth day in February, after the epic blizzard, when the sale more likely happened. But it's remarkable – and entirely fitting – that a fog had set around the truth of the matter so relatively soon after the sale.

Recipients of the card were not only JAM's usual mailing list, but also a few special invitees, like Richard Serra, who may or may not have recognized the invitation as Hammons's rubbing salt into an old wound; the exhibition took place, after all, only a few years after *Shoe Tree* and *Pissed Off.* On view at 503 Broadway was a single snowball that Hammons had apparently kept in a freezer for the three years since the original sale. And just as there had been nothing haphazard about the original display of his snowballs on their rug in 1983, at JAM, Hammons carefully orchestrated his presentation while lending it an air of slight negligence and improvisation. He presented the snowball in an old refrigerator-freezer that he brought into JAM's ex-sweatshop-turned-studio-and-event-space, which was undergoing renovation at the time and had wires dangling amid strewn piles of rubble. When visitors opened the appliance's door, they saw a clear Plexiglas cover that the artist had rigged to the upper freezer compartment in place of its interior door, so that anyone looking in could easily see his carefully preserved specimen. Visitors to Hammons's 'first solo exhibition in ten years' remember that there was nothing on view by the artist except that lone appliance balanced somewhat precariously on top of a mound of rubble and dirt. The single item inside was not perfectly formed anymore, it was a snowball that registered the wear acquired in its move from street to hand to freezer to hand to JAM, and wherever else it might have been in between. As Bey recalls:

> *It was very ugly. I mean, the whole thing was so ugly. ... But to see it again was the experience.* [imitating Hammons's voice] *'I'm gonna show you somethin'.' And then you open it up, and you're like, 'What the hell is that?' Cause it was old, it was dirty, it was funky, it wasn't pristine. But it was the surviving snowball.*[221]

It has been said that Hammons stored one, or perhaps a few, of his 1983 snowballs in various freezers over the years.[222] We know that in 1986 at least one snowball had survived. Or, more precisely, a snowball was *made to* survive. Its maker had wanted to keep a part of *Bliz-aard Ball Sale* safely stowed – for years. While installing 'Icestallation', a snapshot was taken with the remnant snowball. It was positioned, uncooled, in the midst of the space's wall studs and building materials, with Hammons staging it, his forearm caught in the picture, offering a rare glimpse of the relic. It appears, uncommented upon, as an illustration alongside Hammons's interview with Kellie Jones in *Real Life Magazine* (fig.70). To the only journalist that seems to have asked about it at the time, Guy Trebay writing for *The Village Voice*, Hammons explained that although it was a three-year-old, five-inch snowball, three hundred dollars had been spent to present it.[223] Something that had once been for sale for a dollar, and went unsold, was nevertheless worthy of care and display and considerable cost: he was making that point.

There was no denying that 'Icestallation' was important to Hammons, who himself had proposed the unsolicited show to Goode Bryant. And the various choreographers, musicians and photographers occupying the spaces at JAM at the time evidently knew that the aged snowball was dear to him. So, when one night a musician from the Black Rock Coalition, whose members and friends were rehearsing in the building (including Arthur Jafa, Vernon Reid and Greg Tate), inadvertently unplugged the refrigerator-freezer and only discovered the error some time later, pandemonium ensued. Hammons was not someone you wanted to piss off. But more than that, no one wanted to be the person responsible for the destruction of the object the artist had so preciously held on to for years – likely the only remaining trace of his 1983 action. Reid, who admits to having accidently pulled the plug, realized what he had done and got the group to frantically attempt to find another freezer in the building. One can imagine the almost Buster Keaton-esque scene of running back and forth trying to save a snowball. They finally stuffed it in a photographer's mini-freezer compartment after removing his stored film stock. The snowball probably lost some circumference, and maybe it was further dirtied in the process, but it was saved.[224]

Hammons was not amused when he heard the story.[225] Yet it's hard to know why he kept a single, scruffy snowball all that time, why he brought it out for exhibition when he did, or why it mattered so much to him that it might have melted away the night the freezer was accidentally unplugged. The three-year-old testament to his ephemeral street action was not for sale, just for show, and maybe even just to fuel more stories about that winter day when the artist sold snowballs on the street and called it art. Even harder to know than why Hammons presented that remaining snowball, is what happened to it afterward. Not one of the people involved in setting up the show nor who visited it nor those close to Hammons could say for certain where the snowball went after its strange coronation in 'Icestallation'. (Nor how it went – carried in a cooler? transported by hand? stuffed into a jacket pocket?) Nor if it continues to exist at all. Hammons himself refuses to say.

It is this ghosting along with *Bliz-aard Ball Sale*'s afterlife that might be the linchpin to the powerful place the piece occupies in our imaginary – what Seth Price would call an artwork's 'dispersion ... into discourse'.[226] A bit like Duchamp's *Fountain*, which was lost or accidently broken or deliberately smashed or taken almost as soon as it had been chosen from its appliance showroom, never to be seen again, Hammons's last snowball effectively vanished from sight. Duchamp had mastered the art of almost single-handedly ensuring that a quickly lost (but nevertheless documented) urinal would become forever after the stuff of myth-making. Never one to follow a model to the letter, Hammons had his own take on the strategy. From early on he announced to the world that he had a long game in mind - he was no sprinter interested in the flash of quick glory, but was instead 'a long distance runner'.[227] Thus, if Hammons's snowy street-corner sales action has become his most legendary and oft-cited work, it is partly because the artist released just enough, and withheld just enough, of its traces to allow it - like the most salacious of rumours - to spread, shift, grow and get retold again, its details becoming more colourful with each telling.

There is a final afterlife, or maybe just the last of the work's lives as of this writing. In 2016, as part of a survey show at Mnuchin Gallery in New York, representing 'five decades' of his career, Hammons evoked *Bliz-aard Ball Sale* through an installation that was explicitly not for sale: *Untitled (Snowball)* (1983/2003) comprised a frosted glass ball on a small stand with a framed document next to it (fig.71). Hammons thus didn't represent his most iconic artwork via a photographic reproduction clipped from a book or magazine (as he did to represent other ephemeral works in the exhibition), but instead evoked it through an object that visibly refused to act as the original. The document positioned by the glass ball was a framed 2003 fax from Hammons's daughter Carmen to her father. It reproduced an email she had received from a collector couple (their names redacted) who had wanted to purchase a snowball made by the artist. They don't end up going forward with their intended offer: 'as much as we would love to own a snowball', they explain, 'not a single insurance company would cover it for us, and we called half a dozen'.[228] Given this, they 'will have to pass'.

The snowball in question would have been a new one. What mattered to the prospective owners was that it was conceptually connected to the historically significant 1983 sale. It seems that Hammons had not actually agreed to sell a snowball to the couple, but since they wanted (as they admit now) to 'possess a piece of art history', they were in discussions with the artist's daughter to try to convince him.[229] They overlooked the fact that, had it come to pass, insuring the snowball would have forced exactly the permanent legacy, either material or economic, that the ephemeral work

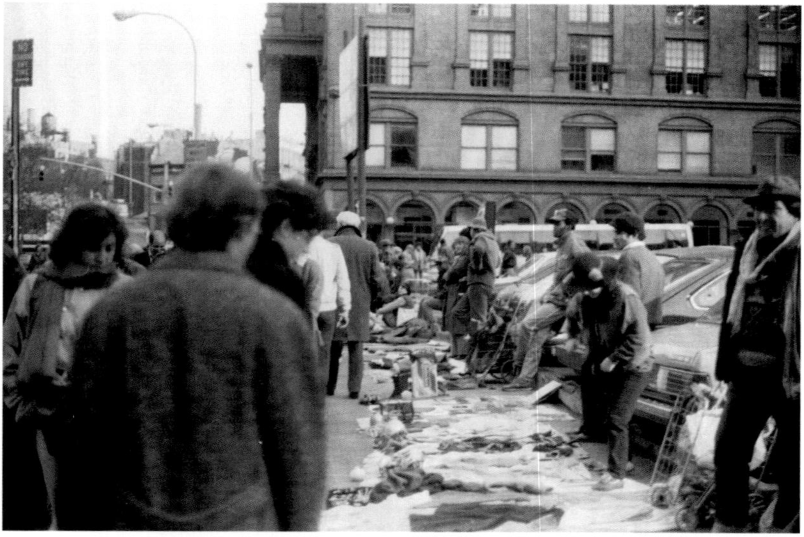

64. Street vendors selling their wares,
Cooper Square and East 8th Street,
New York, c.1984
Photograph and courtesy Susan Fensten

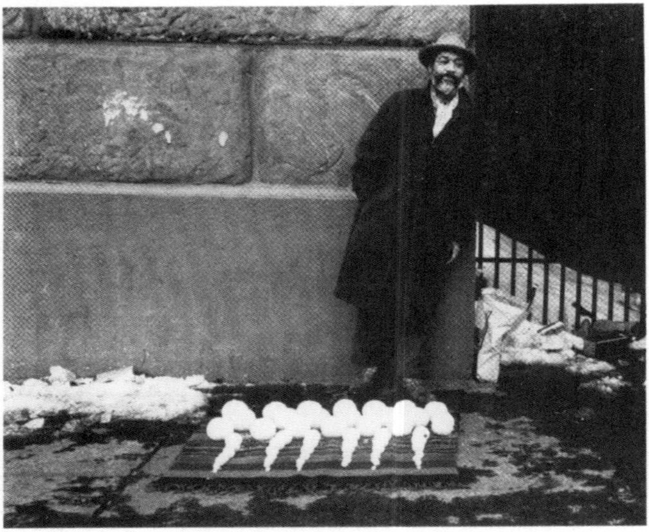

65. David Hammons,
Bliz-aard Ball Sale postcard (recto),
c.1983-89 with photograph by Dawoud Bey
Courtesy Exit Art Archives,
Fales Library and Special Collections,
New York University

Street Vendor Selling Snowballs
Performance by David Hammons, 1983
Photograph by Dawoud Bey

66. David Hammons,
Bliz-aard Ball Sale postcard (verso),
c.1983-89
Courtesy Exit Art Archives,
Fales Library and Special Collections,
New York University

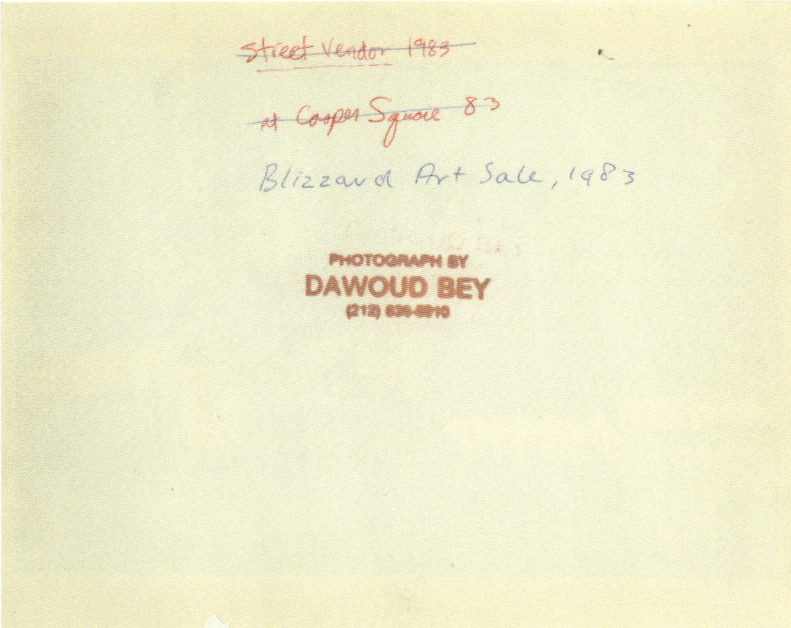

67. Verso of a photograph by Dawoud Bey of *Bliz-aard Ball Sale*, printed and annotated c.1985
Courtesy Exit Art Archives, Fales Library and Special Collections, New York University

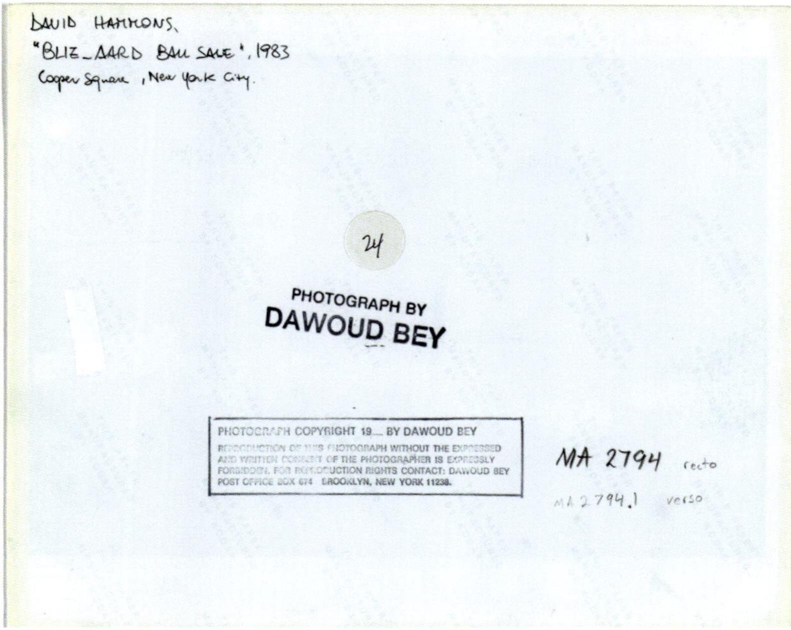

68. Verso of a photograph by Dawoud Bey of *Bliz-aard Ball Sale*, printed and annotated c.1990. Courtesy MoMA P.S.1 Archives, II.A.794, Museum of Modern Art, New York. Digital image © 2022, The Museum of Modern Art, New York/Scala, Florence

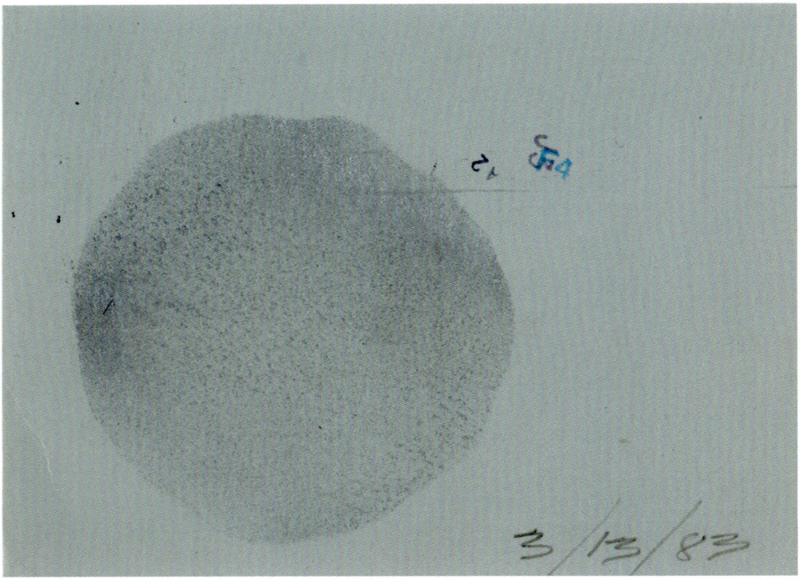

69. David Hammons,
'Icestallation' invitation (recto), 1986
Courtesy Museum of Modern Art, New York

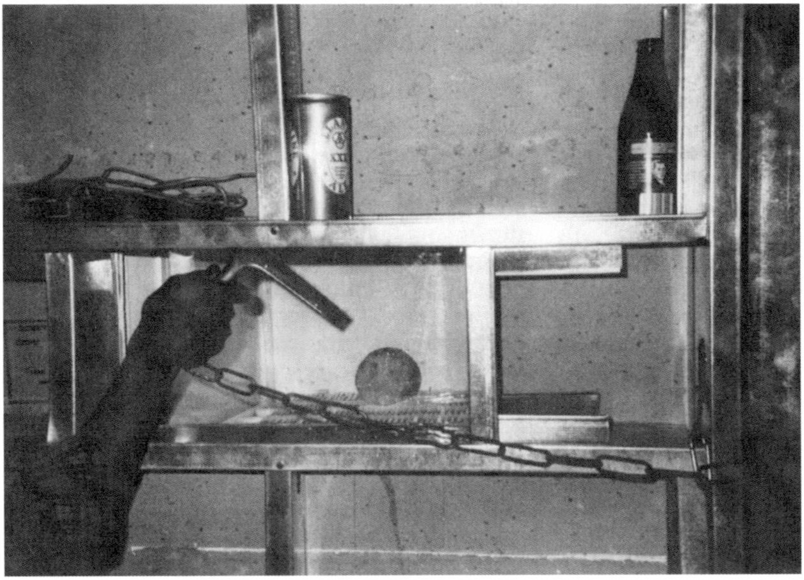

70. View of snowball during
David Hammons's 'Icestallation'
preparations, reproduced in
Real Life Magazine, 1986
Courtesy *Real Life Magazine* Archives,
New York

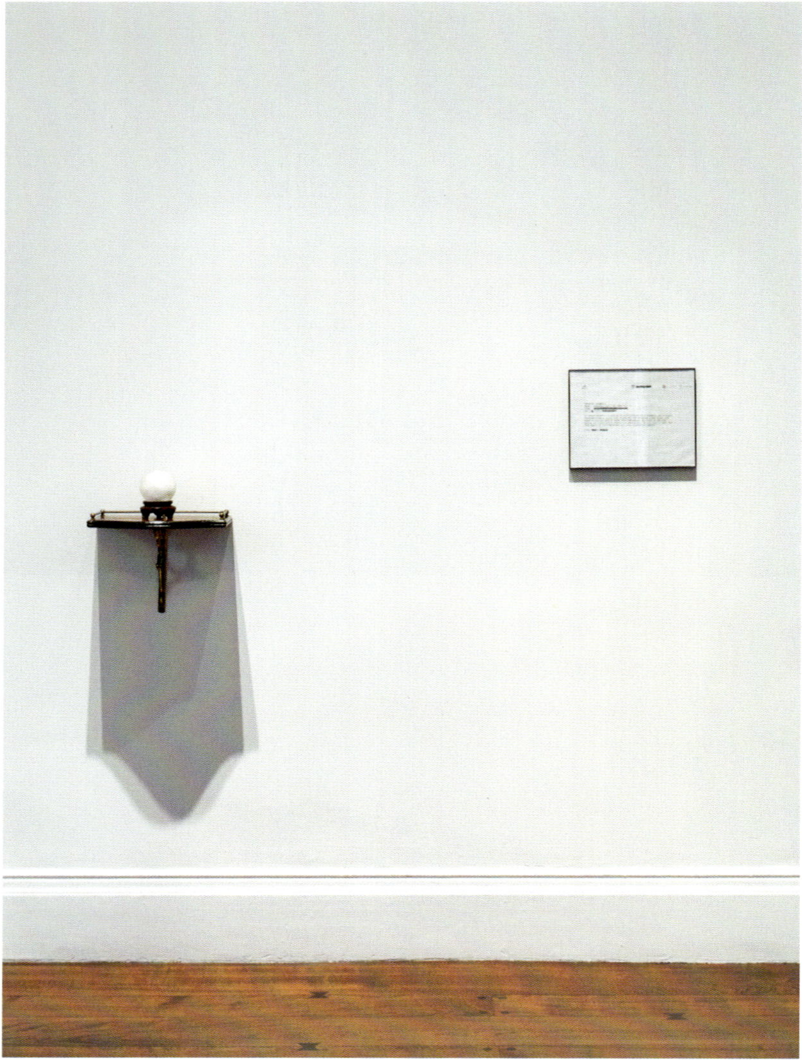

71. Installation view,
David Hammons, *Untitled (Snowball)*,
1983/2003,
in ‘David Hammons: Five Decades’,
Mnuchin Gallery, New York, 2016
Courtesy Mnuchin Gallery

had all along eschewed. Ironically, the collectors' communication confessed to a further reason why the Hammons's work wouldn't be bought: they had taken on debt to remodel their kitchen – presumably one including a state-of-the-art freezer. With sardonic humour, the artist exhibited not only the evidence of the art market's desire to fix him and his work, but also that same market's inability to deal with art that doesn't behave like a conventional (insurable) financial investment.

A few weeks before the exhibition's closing, just as the Frieze New York art fair and the international art world that inevitably attends it arrived in town, Hammons made some adjustments, swapping out items. He replaced the frosted glass ball of *Untitled (Snowball)* with a small glass bowl of water (the fax remained). It was as if his 'snowball' had disappeared into watery obliteration. For this lover of puns, he could hardly have resisted 'unfreezing' his snowball just as the city was being overtaken by visitors to Frieze. Percussive and humorous, as always, Hammons wanted to show the stylish set that they had missed out on something, arrived too late. It was his way, quite simply, of giving the art world the cold shoulder.

What It Is

What I try to do is talk in confusions so when I leave here nothing was really said. It all comes back to nothingness.

– David Hammons[230]

I cannot say I know exactly what Hammons's *Bliz-aard Ball Sale* was – or is. Performance/artwork/exhibition/rumour/public sale/linguistic game/photo shoot/mirror held up to a racist society: it defies and spans several categories at once, and no single descriptor seems to define it adequately. Between action and object, hearsay and photographic record, Hammons's *Bliz-aard Ball Sale* ineluctably raises some of the most fundamental questions about the nature of the work of art. To attend to *Bliz-aard Ball Sale* is to conclude that it is ultimately *unknowable*; in that sense, it has refused, utterly, to become a commodity – a commodity of consumer speculation or of museal preservation, or even of (art-historical) knowledge.

Because the inescapable fact is this (and perhaps this is the only fact about which I am certain with regard to Hammons): even if the truth of *Bliz-aard Ball Sale* remains as elusive as the artist himself, in it lies a political, economic, social and cultural critique that is the backbone of a radical artistic oeuvre. Reminding us of the stakes of Hammons's larger body of work, *Bliz-aard Ball Sale* transforms notions such as 'art', 'commodity', 'performance', 'exhibition' and even 'race' into categories that shift and dissolve, much like slowly melting snowballs.

Such dissolve hasn't always made those snowballs the ready stuff of History with a capital H, which has suited Hammons just fine.[231] 'Do you care about history, in relation to how your work is talked about?' I once asked him. 'No, no, no', he answered. 'I'm more interested in storytelling than in history. There's too much history. We need more mystery!' When I prodded him with regard to *Bliz-aard Ball Sale*'s impermanence, his response was: 'Well, you know, *we're* very impermanent. We are not here that long. [A snowball] goes against bronze sculptures and all of this stuff that is supposed to last.'[232] An ephemeral action, involving a fleeting substance, documented by relatively marginal evidence – everything points to it not having been made to last. Except it did. So, when I later asked the artist if he deliberately cultivates rumours, he said, 'Well, I don't have any control over rumour' – coyly implying that he might not be at the root of the stories that circulate around (or even *as*) his work, while simultaneously suggesting that rumours are more likely to endure than steel or bronze. 'Rumours live a very long time.'[233]

Mystery, rumours, gossip, history, secrets, lies. It is perhaps fitting that a book on *Bliz-aard Ball Sale* would end with doubt about their difference. This, then, has been just one of many possible accounts of *Bliz-aard Ball Sale*, which is to say, an assemblage of research, rumours, hypotheses and provisional conclusions as unstable as ice. Because even after I gathered countless accounts and exhausted every lead, Hammons suggested that, maybe, the attempt to write about *Bliz-aard Ball Sale* (and to suppose that it could be written about at all) was in vain. 'I think you should keep interviewing people', he advised as we walked together on my last visit with him. 'We should keep speaking, you should keep asking questions and researching and continuing to collect your stories. You should keep doing it for years. But then you shouldn't write your book. There would be *no reason* to write the book. Don't you know, chasing these stories is what it *is*?'[234]

1 Quoted in Peter Schjeldahl, 'The Walker: Rediscovering New York with David Hammons', *The New Yorker*, 23 December 2002.

2 On my first meeting with the artist, on 7 September 2009, Hammons refused to respond to my prodding about *Bliz-aard Ball Sale*. But after several hours of walking and as a way to signal the end of our meeting, he nodded to a plot of cement on Cooper Square to which he had led me: 'It happened *there*.' After that, silence. It would take at least five years before he would agree to speak to me again, and then it was perhaps only because he knew that in the interim I had tracked down and interviewed more than forty people connected to him or *Bliz-aard Ball Sale*. Given the ephemeral nature of that work, and given that the people who saw it or knew Hammons at the time had so rarely, if ever, been asked to tell their story, the compilation of an oral history seemed imperative. So, too, did the fervour with which I researched its images, since one pronouncement he had made during that first meeting was the following (it acted as a gauntlet): 'people are lazy, they always tell the same story and reproduce the same few images'. In the citations that follow, I have striven to remain faithful to the original diction and wording of the speakers.

3 The event's date has never been mentioned in discussions of the project, nor could any of those interviewed be pinned down about it.

4 The details shift, even from the same teller. Hammons himself has described the event as taking thirty minutes on one occasion and three hours on another. David Hammons, conversations with the author, New York, 7 September 2009 and 29 September 2015. Dawoud Bey has speculated that it took the whole of a day, having started before he arrived at the scene around noon and continuing until sundown. Most people close to the artist have vehemently insisted that Hammons would not have repeated the act (it simply wouldn't be like him to do so, they've observed). But variations abound: the biography of a catalogue for his recent career survey asserts that he performed the piece 'at various points over the winter'. *David Hammons: Five Decades* (exh. cat.), New York: Mnuchin Gallery, 2016, p.127.

5 Candida Alvarez, Dawoud Bey's partner at the time who accompanied Bey to the sale, has said that freezers were used for storing the snowballs before the day of the sale, and that they were afterwards transported by Hammons in a shopping cart. C. Alvarez, Skype conversation with the author, with the assistance of Alhena Katsof, 5 August 2014.

6 Not knowing (or remembering) how Hammons made them, Bey further ventured that the snowballs were his most meticulously 'crafted' objects. D. Bey, conversation with the author, with the assistance of A. Katsof, New York, 17 July 2014.

7 Hammons recalled, speaking by telephone on 21 August 2014, that he made them on the spot.

8 The one dollar price was cited by Hammons in conversation with the author (New York, 7 September 2009); repeated by Angela Valeria, who attended the sale, in conversation with the author (New York, 11 March 2014); and mentioned in Guy Trebay, 'Pole Vault', *The Village Voice*, 13 May 1986, p.73.

9 Horace Brockington, a curator and friend of Hammons, recalls varying prices, from mere pennies to ten dollars, and the poet Steven Cannon, founder of A Gathering of the Tribes, where Hammons often hung out in New York, insists that each snowball was ten dollars. Conversations with the author, with the assistance of A. Katsof, New York, 4 August 2014 and 28 May 2014, respectively.

10 D. Bey, conversation with the author, with the assistance of A. Katsof, New York, 17 July 2014.

11 D. Hammons, conversation with the author, New York, 7 September 2009.

12 Quoted in J.B., 'Conversing with David Hammons', *ART*, January 2012, p.6, available at http://images.mnuchingallery.com/www_mnuchingallery_com/ARTmagazine_David_Hammons.pdf (last accessed on 12 July 2017).

13 Léopold Sédar Senghor, *Liberté 5*, Paris: Editions du Seuil, 1993. Quoted in Manthia Diawara, '"Dak"Art 2004 Sheep Raffle', in Salah M. Hassan and Cheryl Finley (ed.), *Diaspora, Memory, Place: David Hammons, Maria Magdalena Campos-Pons, Pamela Z*, Munich: Prestel Verlag, 2008, p.145.

14 'The fact is, David's not a hermit at all. He goes to exhibitions. He knows exactly what's going on in the art world. He is no J.D. Salinger hidden someplace.' Horace Brockington, conversation with the author, with the assistance of A. Katsof, New York, 4 August 2015.

15 Conversation with the author, New York, 29 September 2015.

16 D. Bey, 'David Hammons: Purely an Artist', *Uptown*, 1982, p.16.

17 Ralph Ellison, *Invisible Man*, New York: Random House, 1952, p.1. Josine Ianco-Starrels, curator of Hammons's first institutional monographic show, 'David Hammons: Selected Works 1968-1974', in 1974 at California State University, Los Angeles, recounts: 'The first thing David Hammons did, the day after I invited him to have a solo show, was to turn off his phone.' In order to reach him she would have to sit and wait outside his studio. See J. Ianco-Starrels, 'Some Thoughts', in Connie Rogers Tilton and Lindsay Charlwood (ed.), *L.A. Object and David Hammons Body Prints* (exh. cat.), New York: Tilton Gallery, 2011, pp.136-37.

18 D. Hammons, conversation with the author, New York, 7 September 2009. The gaping discrepancies Hammons encountered early in his career between the attention, monetary value and reputation attributed to white versus minority artists by the institutions that supported them can't be emphasized enough. Nor can it be ignored that it remains a reality in the US today.

19 Hammons has never been afraid of being non-compliant. At approximately the same time as shutting down plans for that museum retrospective, he allowed for major survey exhibitions of his work to be organized at an Upper East Side commercial gallery specializing in the secondary market and run by a former equity trader (Mnuchin Gallery) and in the bland corporate headquarters of a Greek shipping magnate and private collector in Athens (Georges Economou Collection) whose name bears etymological relations to 'economy'. None of the implications of each context would have been lost on Hammons. An astute observer of how value is constructed and the market maneuvered, Hammons might even have accepted to do the exhibitions at these two venues precisely because they defied expectation and made a spectacle of his interest in the functioning of the market. 'David Hammons: Five Decades', Mnuchin Gallery, New York and 'Give Me a Moment', Georges Economou Collection, Athens (both 2016).

20 Quoted in Robert Farris Thompson, 'David Hammons: "Knowing their Past"', *Aesthetic of the Cool: Afro-Atlantic Art and Music*, Pittsburgh and New York: Periscope Publishing and Prestel Publishing, 2011, p.100.

21 James Baldwin, 'The Black Boy Looks at the White Boy' (1961), *James Baldwin Collected Essays* (ed. Toni Morrison), New York: Library of America, 1998, p.279.

22 Quoted in Glenn Ligon, 'Black Light: David Hammons and the Poetics of Emptiness', *Artforum*, vol.43, no.1, September 2004, p.249.

23 After noticing this and wondering what caused it (typos? editorial sloppiness? Hammons's own imprecision?), I saw it pointed out in Elvan Zabunyan's excellent *Black is a Color: A History of African American Art* (Paris: Editions Dis Voir, 2005) and started to understand these inconsistencies as systemic and even strategic for Hammons.

24 The cards were written by Sarita Hudgins and reproduced in *Will/Power: New Works by Papo Colo, Jimmie Durham, David Hammons, Hachivi Edgar Heap of Birds, Adrian Piper, and Aminah Brenda Lynn Robinson* (exh. cat.), Columbus, OH: Wexner Center for the Arts, 1993.

25 D. Hammons, quoted in Amei Wallach, 'Pickup Games', *Newsday*, 23 December 1990, p.22.

26 Angela Valeria, conversation with the author, Brooklyn, 30 September 2015.

27 Quoted in A. Wallach, 'Pickup Games', *op. cit.*, p.22.

28 See Hammons's statements in Merrell Noden, 'A Very High Form of Art', *Sports Illustrated*, vol.73, no.26, 24 December 1990.

29 'Interview with David Hammons' (conducted by K. Jones), *Real Life Magazine*, vol.16, Autumn 1986, p.3; reprinted in K. Jones, *EyeMinded: Living and Writing Contemporary Art*, Durham, NC: Duke University Press, 2011, p.248.

30 Published in 1983, Robert Farris Thompson's study became a guidebook of sorts for Hammons; it mined a history of forms to which the artist wanted to connect his own work. See R.F. Thompson, *Flash of the Spirit: African and Afro-American Art and Philosophy*, New York: Random House, 1983. See also R.F. Thompson, 'David Hammons: Soldier in the Army of Harlem's History', written c.1991, unpublished typescript housed in the Exit Art Archives (series I, box 19, folders 31 and 35), Fales Library and Special Collections, New York University, unpaginated; parts of which were later revised and published in R.F. Thompson, 'David Hammons: "Knowing their Past"', *op cit.*, pp.92-105.

31 *Ibid.*, p.93. This has been further explored by Dawoud Bey, who studied with Thompson at Yale and has drawn connections between Hammons's work and African culture. See D. Bey, 'In the Spirit of *Minkisi*: The Art of David Hammons', *Third Text*, vol.8, issue 27, 1994, pp.45-54.

32 Recounted by A.C. Hudgins, conversation with the author, New York, 21 March 2016.

33 Recounted by A. Valeria, conversation with the author, Brooklyn, 30 September 2015.

34 See R.F. Thompson, 'David Hammons: "Knowing their Past"', *op cit.*, p.95.

35 In Ulysses Jenkins's 1978 film on Hammons, *King David*, the artist's 'private studies' with White are listed alongside his more official enrolment in various places of higher education.

36 See Joseph E. Young, 'Three Graphic Artists', in *Three Graphic Artists: Charles White, David Hammons, Timothy Washington* (exh. cat.), Los Angeles: Los Angeles County Museum of Art, 1971, p.7.

37 Suzanne Jackson, telephone conversation with the author, with the assistance of A. Katsof, 21 May 2016.

38 It would be tempting to imagine that much of this has changed in the intervening decades, but as I write this, the white supremacy that propels what is taking place at this very moment is uncannily comparable with the white supremacy that propelled what happened then. This, too, is the ongoing backdrop of Hammons's practice.

39 Quoted in R.F. Thompson, 'David Hammons: "Knowing their Past"', *op cit.*, p.95. See also the description of Hammons's process and use of contradictory signs in L. Goode Bryant and Marcy S. Philips, *Contextures*, New York: Just Above Midtown, 1978, pp.40-41.

40 Hammons's statement is cited in Samella Lewis and Ruth Waddy (ed.), *Black Artists on Art*, vol.1, Los Angeles: Contemporary Crafts, 1971, p.21. He repeated the statement, almost verbatim, to Lynne Cooke. See L. Cooke, 'Yo', *Parkett*, vol.32, March 1992, p.47.

41 The events in LA prompted Hammons's 'juxtaposition of black people against the American flag', as he recounted to Charlie Ahearn. See C. Ahearn, '"Tragic Magic" Sparks Hammons Retrospective at P.S.1', *The City Sun*, 16-22 January 1991. For an in-depth discussion of these works, see K. Jones, 'Good Mirrors Ain't Cheap', *David Hammons: Five Decades* (exh. cat.), New York: Mnuchin Gallery, 2016, pp.15-18.

42 In 1992, Hammons told R.F. Thompson: 'It was always a very accurate stamp, never like an Yves Klein. ... And by using my own body, it definitely became black art.' Quoted in R.F. Thompson, 'David Hammons: "Knowing their Past"', *op cit.*, p.95.

43 See U. Jenkins's documentary *King David*, from 1978.

44 'Interview with David Hammons' (conducted by K. Jones), *op. cit.*, p.249.

45 Such is the astute reading in R.F. Thompson, 'David Hammons: "Knowing their Past"', *op. cit.*, p.103.

46 'Interview with David Hammons' (conducted by K. Jones), *op. cit.*, p.249.

47 *Ibid.*

48 Manthia Diawara, 'Make it Funky: The Art of David Hammons', *Artforum*, vol.36, no.9, May 1998, p.126.

49 See K. Jones, 'Black West, Thoughts on Art in LA', *op. cit.*, p.59.

50 Quoted in G. Trebay, 'Pole Vault', *op. cit.*, p.73.

51 'You Have to be Prepared: A Conversation Between David Hammons and Robert Storr', in *Yardbird Suite: Hammons 93* (exh. cat.), Williamstown, MA: Williams College Museum of Art, 1994, p.56.

52 For more on this still largely unwritten history, see Carolyn Peter and Damon Willick, 'Suzanne Jackson's Gallery 32 and Los Angeles's Burgeoning African American

Arts Community', *nka*, vol.30, 2012, pp.16-27; and K. Jones, 'Now Dig This! An Introduction', in *Now Dig This! Art and Black Los Angeles 1960-1980* (exh. cat.), Los Angeles: Hammer Museum, University of California, 2011, pp.20-21.

53 Thompson's university lectures and early published studies on the concepts of control and composure found in West African and Afro-American rituals, music and dance, made him, according to a 1984 article in *Rolling Stone*, the father of the 'Canons of the Cool'. See Fred Iseman, 'Robert Farris Thompson: Canons of the Cool', *Rolling Stone*, 22 November 1984, available at http://www.rollingstone.com/culture/features/canons-of-the-cool-19841122 (last accessed on 12 July 2017).

54 G. Ligon, 'Notes on a Performance by Kellie Jones', in Triple Canopy and Ralph Lemon (ed.), *On Value*, New York: Triple Canopy, 2015, p.70.

55 Steve Cannon, quoted in Courtney Willis Blair, 'Trickster Aesthetics', *Modern Painters*, vol.28, no.4, 5 April 2016, pp.62-69.

56 Mentioned by Hammons and the film-maker in U. Jenkins's film *King David*.

57 See Barry Maxwell, 'Chromatic Shadows, So What? Notes Toward Better Understanding of David Hammons's Signals', in S.M. Hassan and C. Finley (ed.), *Diaspora, Memory, Place*, *op. cit.*, p.170.

58 Ralph Ellison, 'Richard Wright's Blues', *Living with Music: Ralph Ellison's Jazz Writings* (ed. Robert G. O'Meally), New York: Modern Library, 2001, p.103.

59 D. Hammons in interview no.1 with Papo Colo and Jeanette Ingberman (1989), typescript housed in Exit Art Archives (series I, box 19, folders 33 and 35), Fales Library and Special Collections, New York University, p.1.

60 'Interview with David Hammons' (conducted by K. Jones), *op. cit.*, p.249. The sales price of *The Wine Leading the Wine* is mentioned in R.F. Thompson, 'David Hammons: "Knowing their Past"', *op. cit.*, p.95.

61 'Interview with David Hammons' (conducted by K. Jones), *op. cit.*, p.248.

62 Quoted in L. Goode Bryant and M.S. Philips, *Contextures*, *op. cit.*, p.41. Goode Bryant opened her now-legendary Just Above Midtown gallery in November 1974 at 50 West 57th Street as the first commercial art gallery in New York focused on black artists and one, moreover, that dared to operate in the elite midtown gallery district. Her relentless commitment to and role in the early promotion of Hammons's work as well as that of Senga Nengudi, Lorraine O'Grady, Fred Wilson and others should not be underestimated.

63 So much fervour ensued that JAM spontaneously organized a public discussion about the matter. Recounted by L. Goode Bryant to the author, New York, 2 October 2015.

64 Recounted by A.C. Hudgins to the author, New York, 29 September 2015.

65 'David Hammons: Greasy Bags and Barbecue Bones' (5-31 May 1975), 'David Hammons: Dreadlock Series' (6-26 April 1976) and 'David Hammons: Recent Hair Sculpture' (29 March-16 April 1977), all at Just Above Midtown Gallery, New York. For the most sustained discussion of Hammons's use of hair, see 'In the Thick of It: David Hammons and Hair Culture in the 1970s' and 'Brothers and Sisters', in K. Jones, *EyeMinded*, *op. cit.*, pp.297-304 and 460-467, respectively.

66 So much was this the case that it created a problem for the preparation of his first retrospective, 'Rousing the Rubble' (P.S.1 Contemporary Art Center, New York; 16 December 1990-10 February 1991). Because most of his early greasy bag, hair and barbecue pieces had been thrown away, lost or destroyed (few had ever sold), Hammons had to reconstruct them.

67 Hammons is said to have once had a rule that his art shouldn't cost him more than eight dollars to put together. Neighbourhood trash bins were his most fruitful supply source. The choice reflects the economic disparity that has historically divided black and white communities. After all, there are certain kinds of garbage more likely to be found on Harlem's Frederick Douglass Boulevard than Park Avenue. Garbage carries cultural traces of the communities that produce it, and the economic and racial divisions that have been re-enforced by administrative neglect on the part of governmental authorities. A decided social and cultural critique thus lies in what kinds of 'garbage' Hammons has chosen to appropriate, from hair clippings and Thunderbird wine bottles, in his early work, to fur coats and antique armoires, more recently. Shifts in the artist's material choices, level of craftmanship and positioning in relation to race are fascinatingly significant and under-discussed, meriting an additional essay.

68 On Hammons's influences, see D. Bey, 'In the Spirit of *Minkisi*: The Art of David Hammons', *op. cit.*, pp.45-54.

69 Hammons insistently cites the French artist's work and has explicitly appropriated his tactics. To name just a few of many examples: Hammons's presentation of urinals on trees in a Belgian forest (*Public Toilets*, 1990); his artist's edition *Holy Bible: The Old Testament* (2002), comprised of gilt-edged, leather-bound 'black face' copies of Arturo Schwarz's monograph *The Complete Works of Marcel Duchamp* (1969), which literally claims a Duchampian lineage while simultaneously taking over authorship from both artist and art historian; his repeated attempts over the years to have art institutions close their premises and stop work on 28 July in honour of Duchamp's birthday, so as to (sardonically) promote the artist as the art-world saint he is; and his repeated declaration that he is 'the C.E.O. of the D.O.C. - the Duchamp Outpatient Clinic'.

70 See Duchamp's advice to artists in 'Where Do We Go from Here?', delivered in March 1961 at a symposium at the Philadelphia Museum College of Art. Helen Meakins's translation was published in *Studio International*, vol.189, January/February 1975, p.28.

71 'Interview with David Hammons' (conducted by Maurice Berger), *Art in America*, vol.78, no.9, September 1990, p.80.

72 As late as 1990, Hammons noted: 'I have one patron, A.C. Hudgins. He has been buying my work for over fifteen years. He is a black person who lives on 163rd Street in upper Manhattan. He's been my only patron. He lends me money, and I'll pay it back with a piece, or he'll buy something to keep me going.' *Ibid.*, p.80.

73 These included, between 1981-93: a grant from the Studio Museum Harlem (1981); a National Endowment for the Arts Fellowship (1983-84); a New York State Council on the Arts Award (1983-84); a Guggenheim Memorial Foundation Award (1983-84); an Art Matters Award, from the New York Foundation for the Arts (1987); a Tiffany Grant (1990); the Prix de Rome for Sculpture, from the American Academy in Rome (1990/1991); the Brendan Gill Award of the Municipal Art Society (1991); and a MacArthur Foundation Fellowship (1991).

74 See J. Ianco-Starrels, 'Some Thoughts', *op. cit.*, pp.136-37; and Alanna Heiss, 'My Friend David Hammons', in *David Hammons: Five Decades*, *op. cit.*, p.13.

75 See Tom Finkelpearl's recollections in 'Call Me Galaxie: Tom Finkelpearl and Thomas J. Lax In Conversation', in Triple Canopy and R. Lemon (ed.), *On Value, op. cit.*, p.108.

76 D. Hammons, quoted in Amei Wallach, 'Rubble-Rouser', *Los Angeles Times*, 18 August 1991, available at http://articles.latimes.com/1991-08-18/entertainment/ca-1418_1_david-hammons (last accessed on 12 July 2017).

77 Hammons installed the damaged work indoors shortly after, in late 1990, as part of 'Rousing the Rubble' at P.S.1 Contemporary Art Center, where he showed it surrounded by a parody of museum stanchions built from wire and a row of sledgehammers, one with a box of Lucky Strike cigarettes attached.

78 A.C. Hudgins, conversation with the author, New York, 29 September 2015.

79 Although P.S.1's *Rousing the Rubble*, published in 1991, is Hammons's first monograph, P. Colo and J. Ingberman collected photographic material on Hammons's past works, conducted multiple interviews with the artist and commissioned essays on him over several years in an attempt to make what would have been a first monographic catalogue on the artist, to commemorate his 1989 exhibition at Exit Art. The grants that were meant to fund it fell through and it ultimately was not published due to lack of funding. Its manuscripts and preparatory materials are located in the Exit Art Archives (series I, box 19, folders 21-36 and series I subseries, box 175, folder 1), Fales Library and Special Collections, New York University. They have been a rich resource for my study.

80 Patrick Pacheco, 'Art Gets Serious with a New Set of Stars', *The New York Times*, 3 March 1991.

81 'I make a definite distinction between that marginality which is imposed by oppressive structures and that marginality one chooses as site of resistance - as location of radical openness and possibility.' bell hooks, 'Choosing the Margin as a Space for Radical Openness', *Yearnings: Race, Gender and Cultural Politics*, Boston: South End Press, 1990, p.153.

82 Stanley Whitney, conversation with the author, with the assistance of A. Katsof, New York, 14 October 2014.

83 The artist Angela Valeria, with whom Hammons was then involved, recalls the endless night walks they would take through the city so that Hammons could check out the sales displays. Conversation with the author, New York, 11 March 2014.

84 'Interview with David Hammons' (conducted by Steve Cannon, Gail Shilke, Jemeel Moondoc, David Henderson and Keith Gilyard), *A Gathering of the Tribes*, Autumn 1991, p.4.

85 D. Bey, conversation with the author, with the assistance of A. Katsof, New York, 17 July 2014.

86 R.F. Thompson, 'David Hammons: "Knowing their Past"', *op. cit.*, p.100.

87 D. Hammons, telephone conversation with the author, 21 August 2014.

88 *Ibid.*

89 Two accounts encapsulate well what those who saw the event have repeatedly noted: 'He placed the balls in lines that followed their scale, he was very particular and very specific. [...] And he stood very straight. He wasn't dancing around or getting people's attention.[...] He stood back and let the action happen on its own terms, allowing time to be a part of it.' C. Alvarez, Skype conversation with the author, with the assistance of A. Katsof, New York, 5 August 2014. And: 'People knew there was something special just from the way he set it up and what he was doing. He was making a point about display.' Danny Dawson, conversation with the author, with the assistance of A. Katsof, New York, 22 April 2015.

90 Jules Allen, conversation with the author, with the assistance of A. Katsof, New York, 25 September 2015.

91 D. Bey, conversation with the author, with the assistance of A. Katsof, New York, 17 July 2014.

92 See Lucy R. Lippard, *Six Years: The Dematerialization of the Art Object from 1966 to 1972*, New York: Praeger, 1973.

93 'Interview with David Hammons' (conducted by K. Jones), *op. cit.*, p.251.

94 After leaving Los Angeles for New York in 1974, he nevertheless visited regularly and for rather lengthy stints through 1978, working in the studio of Senga Nengudi on La Salle Avenue whenever he was in town.

95 Senga Nengudi, conversation with the author, with the assistance of A. Katsof, 13 April 2016.

96 Barbara McCullough's 16mm film *Shopping Bag Spirits and Freeway Fetishes* documents ritual practices in the art of different members of the black art community in Los Angeles.

97 D. Bey, conversation with the author, with the assistance of A. Katsof, New York, 17 July 2014.

98 Many artists lived and worked in that area, and JAM was nearby, making *T.W.U.* a fixture Hammons walked by regularly. Linda Goode Bryant describes having long discussions with Hammons about Serra's work as well as Hammons's announcement that he needed to 'react to' the monument. His riposte was to add the shoes, which she reported he did at night, often throwing a few at a time. Bryant, conversation with the author, New York, 2 October 2015.

99 D. Hammons, telephone conversation with the author, 22 August 2014.

100 D. Hammons, in interview no.1 with P. Colo and J. Ingberman, *op. cit.*, p.12.

101 For instance, Bey's photographs of *Pissed Off*, *Shoe Tree* and *Bliz-aard Ball Sale* seem not to have circulated in print until nearly a decade after they were taken, when they appeared in *David Hammons: Rousing the Rubble* (exh. cat.), New York: P.S.1 Contemporary Art Center, 1990.

102 See K. Jones, 'The Structure of Myth and Potency of Magic', in *ibid.*, p.34; reprinted in *EyeMinded*, *op. cit.*, pp.145-56.

103 This was a practice Hammons avidly read about in his dog-eared copy of R.F. Thompson's *Flash of the Spirit* (*op. cit.*), whose influence on his various 'bottle' works he credits in 'Interview with David Hammons' (conducted by K. Jones, *op. cit.*, pp.258-59).

104 So it was for Hammons's initiation of the project *Art Across the Park*, when he encouraged curators Horace Brockington and Gylbert Coker to invite artists to stage the temporary exhibition of ephemeral, outdoor sculptures in Central Park, which they did in 1980 and 1982, after which Hammons refused be further involved, suggesting that with two editions and public funding the project had become 'too institutionalized'. H. Brockington and G. Coker, conversations with the author, with the assistance of A. Katsof, New York, 4 August 2014 and 26 May 2014, respectively.

105 Hammons called the first piece of the series *Pole Dreams*, anticipating two versions that he named *Higher Goals*: a single pole erected in Harlem in 1983, and a set of five erected in Brooklyn in 1986. See G. Coker, 'Human Pegs, Pole Dreams', *The Village Voice*, 28 September 1982, pp.75-79.

106 'Interview with David Hammons' (by K. Jones), *op. cit.*, p.251.

107 See description in G. Coker, 'Human Pegs, Pole Dreams', *op. cit.*, pp.75-79.

108 Hammons applied for the John Simon Guggenheim Memorial Foundation Fellowship in 1983, the same year as *Bliz-aard Ball Sale* took place, and was awarded the grant the following year. Linda Goode Bryant typed the application out for him, as she or other friends regularly did, and almost fought with Hammons because he insisted, against her advice, on describing his project in a single line of text. L. Goode Bryant, conversation with the author, New York, 2 October 2015.

109 D. Hammons in 'Interview with David Hammons' (by S. Cannon, G. Shilke, J. Moondoc, D. Henderson and K. Gilyard), *op. cit.*, p.5.

110 A single postcard found its way into the Exit Art Archives (series IV subseries, box 175, folder 1), Fales Library and Special Collections, New York University.

111 L. Goode Bryant, conversation with the author, with the assistance of A. Katsof, New York, 5 July 2016.

112 According to a letter included with the images, Bey had printed the images by 1985. Correspondence and photographs housed in the Exit Art Archives (series I, box 19, folder 25 and series IV subseries, box 175, folder 1), Fales Library and Special Collections, New York University.

113 Photographers who have described similar scenarios include Jules Allen, Dawoud Bey, Erma Estwick and Coreen Simpson.

114 See G. Coker, 'Human Pegs, Pole Dreams', *op. cit.*, pp.75-79.

115 André Malraux, *Museum Without Walls: The Psychology of Art* (trans. Stuart Gilbert), New York: Pantheon Books, 1949, pp.28 and 32.

116 S. Nengudi, telephone conversation with the author, with the assistance of A. Katsof, 17 August 2014.

117 At a recent career survey, 'David Hammons: Five Decades' (2016) at Mnuchin Gallery, New York, Hammons referenced his performative practice by showing images as they appeared in magazines or other publications (torn or cut from their source and placed in ill-fitting found frames); refusing the aura of the 'authentic' document (and the snobbery of the art world that privileges it), he offered instead the twice-mediated image.

118 R. Ellison, *Invisible Man*, *op. cit.*, pp.153-54.

119 Quoted by S. Nengudi, telephone conversation with the author, with the assistance of A. Katsof, 17 August 2014.

120 D. Bey, conversation with the author, with the assistance of A. Katsof, New York, 22 May 2015.

121 Quoted in Deborah Menaker Rothschild, 'Reflections of a Long Distance Runner', in *Yardbird Suite: Hammons 93*, *op. cit.*, p.51.

122 Marcel Broodthaers, quoted in Seth Price, *Dispersion* (2006-), unpaginated, available at distributedhistory.com/Dispersion2016.pdf (last accessed on 12 July 2017).

123 Robert Lebel, 'Marcel Duchamp: Whiskers and Kicks of All Kinds', in R. Lebel (ed.), *Marcel Duchamp*, New York: Paragraphic Books, 1959, p.97.

124 See Andrew Russeth, 'Looking at Seeing: David Hammons and the Politics of Visibility', *ArtNews*, 17 February 2015, available at artnews.com/2015/02/17/david-hammons-and-the-politics-of-visibility/ (last accessed on 12 July 2017).

125 Fred Moten, 'To Feel, To Feel More, To Feel More Than', in Rose Bouthillier (ed.), *How To Remain Human* (exh. cat.), Cleveland: Museum of Contemporary Art Cleveland, 2015.

126 For a discussion of the centrality of Duchamp's 'curatorial' role in the positioning of his oeuvre, see my *The Apparently Marginal Activities of Marcel Duchamp*, Cambridge, MA: The MIT Press, 2016.

127 Yve-Alain Bois, 'Ray Guns', in Y-A. Bois and Rosalind E. Krauss, *Formless: A User's Guide*, Cambridge, MA: The MIT Press, 1997, pp.173-76.

128 Steven Stern, 'A Fraction of the Whole', *Frieze*, no.129, March 2009, pp.114-19, available at https://frieze.com/article/fraction-whole (last accessed on 12 July 2017).

129 Quoted in G. Trebay, 'Pole Vault', *op. cit.*, p.73.

130 *Ibid.*

131 'Interview with David Hammons' (by K. Jones), *op. cit.*, p.254.

132 H. Brockington, conversation with the author, with the assistance of A. Kasof, New York, 4 August 2014.

133 Conversation with the author, with the assistance of A. Katsof, New York, 9 August 2014.

134 R.F. Thompson, 'David Hammons: "Knowing their Past"', *op. cit.*, p.94.

135 C. Jennings, conversation with the author, with the assistance of A. Katsof, New York, 9 August 2014.

136 C. Alvarez, Skype conversation with the author, with the assistance of A. Katsof, 5 August 2014.

137 'No Wonder' (D. Hammons interviewed by Louise Neri), *Parkett*, vol.31, March 1992, p.50.

138 D. Hammons, in interview no.2 with P. Colo and J. Ingberman (1989), *op. cit.*, p.15.

139 Tom Finkelpearl, 'Ideology of Dirt', in *David Hammons: Rousing the Rubble, op. cit.*, p.81.

140 Jeanne Rohatyn Greenberg describes Hammons taking a rock home, bathing it and living with it for quite some time before it ultimately became part of his *Rock Head* series. Other objects would sit in his studio for even longer, maybe even a decade, before Hammons would determine that they felt 'right'. J. Rohatyn Greenberg, conversation with the author, New York, 30 September 2015.

141 'Interview with David Hammons' (by S. Cannon, G. Shilke, J. Moondoc, D. Henderson and K. Gilyard), *op. cit.*, p.6.

142 *Ibid.*, p.3.

143 D. Hammons, in interview no.1 with P. Colo and J. Ingberman, *op. cit.*, p.11.

144 For a discussion of value in Hammons's work, see Mark Godfrey, 'Flight Fantasties: On the Work of David Hammons', in *Give Me a Moment* (exh. cat.), Athens: The George Economou Collection, 2016, pp.19-41.

145 D. Bey, conversation with the author, with the assistance of A. Katsof, New York, 17 July 2014.

146 Quoted in Deborah Solomon, 'The Downtowning of Uptown', *The New York Times Magazine*, 19 August 2001.

147 'Malcolm X on the Power of Africa' (20 December 1964), available at http://malcolmxfiles.blogspot.ch/2013/07/at-audubon-ballroom-december-20-1964.html (last accessed on 12 July 2017).

148 Quoted in C. Ahearn, '"Tragic Magic" Sparks Hammons Retrospective at P.S.1', *op. cit.*

149 'Interview with David Hammons' (conducted by K. Jones), *op. cit.*, pp.250-51.

150 Quoted in C. Ahearn, '"Tragic Magic" Sparks Hammons Retrospective at P.S.1', *op. cit.*

151 Tom Finkelpearl, 'Ideology of Dirt', *op. cit.*, p.81.

152 Mary Douglas, *Purity and Danger: An Analysis of Concepts of Pollution and Taboo*, London: Routledge, 1966. Quoted in G. Ligon, 'Notes on a Performance by Kellie Jones', *op. cit.*, 2016, p.74.

153 D. Hammons, quoted in 'No Wonder', *op. cit.*, p.53.

154 'Interview with David Hammons' (conducted by K. Jones), *op. cit.*, p.252.

155 See J. Baldwin, 'A Fly in Buttermilk' (1961), *James Baldwin Collected Essays*, *op. cit.* Originally published as 'The Hard Kind of Courage', *Harper's*, October 1958.

156 Quoted in C. Ahearn, '"Tragic Magic" Sparks Hammons Retrospective at P.S.1', *op. cit.*

157 Greg Tate, 'Dark Angels of Dust: David Hammons and the Art of Streetwise Transcendentalism', in *Art in the Streets* (exh. cat.), Los Angeles: Museum of Contemporary Art, 2011, p.114.

158 He does so all while not letting you forget the piece's connection to the marketplace, as if blizzard + bazaar = Bliz-aard. Coco Fusco and Christian Hale's brilliant discussion of language in Hammons's work emphasizes the power of his punning: 'He is, in actuality, a masterful investigator of how an oppositional black cultural identity can be generated through a dialogue with 'high' culture, particularly as it is articulated through standard English. His method relies on punning and other kinds of word games that short-circuit the dominant cultural interpretation of any given object or term to be redirected for his own purpose.' See C. Fusco and C. Hale, 'Wreaking Havoc on the Signified', *frieze*, no.22, May 1995, pp.34-41.

159 I thank Senam Okudzeto for, among other things, pressing me to look closely at Hammons's posture as a construction, much like Joseph Beuys's.

160 See R.F. Thompson, 'Hammons' Harlem Equation: Four Shots of Memory, Three Shots of Avant Garde', *Parkett*, vol.31, March 1992, p.21.

161 D. Hammons, quoted in *ibid.*

162 See 'Interview with David Hammons' (conducted by K. Jones), *op. cit.*, p.250.

163 This is not to say that such pieces didn't eventually enter collections, but if the complexity of orchestrating their sale and the protracted discussion, for instance, around the Whitney Museum of American Art's purchase of *Untitled* (1992) is any example, it suggests that these were particularly hard sells even when they happened. Conversation with Jack Tilton, New York, 21 March 2016.

164 Conversation with the author, New York, 21 March 2016.

165 *Ibid.*

166 For more on this exhibition, see A. Katsof, 'Colab, *Times Square Show*, 1980', in Elena Filipovic (ed.), *The Artist as Curator: An Anthology*, Milan: Mousse Publishing, 2017, pp.139-158.

167 See the testimonial of Jane Dickson, Colab member and one of the exhibition's organizers, available at timessquareshowrevisited.com/accounts/jane-dickson.html (last accessed on 12 July 2017).

168 See Hammons's description of the piece and glee at the hassle it involved for the gallery in interview no.2 with P. Colo and J. Ingberman, *op. cit.*, pp.6-7.

169 A.C. Hudgins and H. Brockington, conversation with the author, New York, 21 March 2016.

170 F. Moten, 'The Case of Blackness', *Criticism*, vol.50, no.2, Spring 2008, pp.177-218.

171 Hammons notes that fellow black artists often criticized his work because he was revealing cultural secrets and offering a less than favourable image of their culture - 'showing a bad image of Harlem'. See 'Interview with David Hammons' (conducted by K. Jones), *op. cit.*, p.254. See also 'You Have to be Prepared: A Conversation Between David Hammons and Robert Storr', *op. cit.*, p.59.

172 Quoted in A. Wallach, 'Pickup Games', *op. cit.*, p.22.

173 Hammons explicitly refuted making connections between *Bliz-aard Ball Sale* and race issues in conversations with the author on: 7 September 2009, 21 August 2014, 4 September 2014, and 29 September 2015.

174 'Interview with David Hammons' (conducted by M. Berger), *op. cit.*, p.80; 'You Have to be Prepared: A Conversation Between David Hammons and Robert Storr', *op. cit.*, p.58.

175 *Ibid.*

176 Cari Luna, 'Squatters of the Lower East Side', *Jacobin*, 3 April 2014, jacobinmag.com/2014/04/squatters-of-the-lower-east-side/ (last accessed on 12 July 2017).

177 Christopher Mele, *Selling the Lower East Side: Culture, Real Estate, and Resistance in New York City*, Minnesota: University of Minnesota Press, 2000, p.181.

178 *Ibid.*, p.199.

179 See Walter Robinson and Carlo McCormick, 'Slouching Toward Avenue D', *Art in America*, vol.72, no.6, Summer 1984, p.135. In their essay 'The Fine Art of Gentrification', Rosalyn Deutsche and Cara Gendel Ryan chart the numerous articles that were published about the burgeoning scene in the art press between 1982-84, revealing just how much Hammons's 'bliz-aard' had located itself in the eye of the storm. See R. Deutsche and C. Gendel Ryan, 'The Fine Art of Gentrification', *The Portable Lower East Side*, vol.4, no.1, Spring 1987, available at abcnorio.org/about/history/fine_art.html (last accessed on 12 July 2017).

180 See W. Robertson and C. McCormick, 'Slouching Toward Avenue D', *op. cit.*, pp.135-61; and R. Deutsche and C. Gendel Ryan, 'The Fine Art of Gentrification', *op. cit.*, pp.91-111. See also C. Mele, 'Developing the East Village: Eighties Counterculture in the Service of Urban Capital', *Selling the Lower East Side, op. cit.*, pp.220-54.

181 Quoted by Dan Cameron in his statement in 'The 1980s: An Internet Conference' organized by Maurice Berger (31 October-1 November 2005). Practices like that of Jeff Koons acted as a perfect *précis* of the moment, cannily mirroring its rampant commodity fetishism and love of surface, sheen and brand names. That Koons's series of Hoovers were born of this moment is no accident, nor could be the dichotomy between Koons and Hammons more stark.

182 R.F. Thompson, 'David Hammons: "Knowing their Past"', *op. cit.*, p.92.

183 G. Trebay, 'Pole Vault', *op. cit.*, p.73.

184 The First Lady's support of her husband's positions, stoically standing by while an unprecedented number of people went homeless (and an ever-increasing array of designer clothing filled her closets), caused her detractors to protest. As a retort, and with astoundingly little irony, she attended a 1982 Washington DC benefit dressed in tattered garb, suggesting a homeless person or 'bag lady', to shock her detractors out of commenting on her expensive outfits.

185 Greg Tate, 'David Hammons', typescript housed in Exit Art Archives (series I, box 19, folder 32 and 35), Fales Library and Special Collections, New York University, unpaginated.

186 In 1980, 32.5 per cent of African Americans were living in poverty in the US, according to a statistic provided by the Centers for Disease Control and Prevention. See Neil Irwin, Claire Cain Miller and Margot Sanger-Katz, 'America's Racial Divide, Charted', *The New York Times*, 19 August 2014.

187 Kobena Mercer, 'Endangered Species: Danny Tisdale and Keith Piper', *Artforum*, vol.30, no.10, Summer 1992, p.75.

188 While the relationship of black lives to the street in the 1980s inheres in *Bliz-aard Ball Sale*, so, too, does a more distant history in which enslaved Africans were sold on the open market at Wall Street. One (dark) history of street selling did not beget the other. But it would it be a mistake to ignore the shared genealogy between black bodies and commodities sold in the streets of New York, or to ignore how indelibly entrenched this genealogy is in America's history and its psyche (the trafficking of black bodies being the literal material and financial foundation of the US economy).

189 See Frantz Fanon, *Black Skin, White Masks*, New York: Grove Press, 1952. I thank Thomas McDonough for, among other things, suggesting the link between the semantic whiteness of snow and Fanon's reading of race.

190 In 1982, James Q. Wilson and George L. Kelling published their influential essay 'Broken Windows: The Police and Neighbourhood Safety' in *The Atlantic Monthly* (vol.249, no.3, March 1982, pp.29-38). Articulating the prevailing attitude of the time, it posited that putting an end to small crimes - loitering, vandalism, panhandling and public urination - was key to restoring an urban orderliness. The 'Broken Windows Theory' was adopted by New York City Police administrators, and went hand in hand with racial profiling and arrests for non-criminal behaviour in public space.

191 Apocryphally attributed to Malcolm X, but in fact an expression from long before his time, it remained absolutely current in Hammons's era, as evinced by an answer from 'The Ebony Advisor' in the January 1983 issue of *Ebony* (vol.38, no.3, p.78): 'To assume Black colleges are inferior to White colleges is as fallacious as is some people's belief that the White man's ice is colder.' In 1990, several years after the sale, Hammons made the work *Whose Ice Is Colder?*. Comprised of three massive blocks of ice positioned under a South Korean, an African-National and a Yemenite flag, it underscored the kind of everyday racism that persisted amongst Koreans, African Americans and Yemenites in his own neighbourhood. See fig.51.

192 See Teju Cole, 'Black Body: Rereading James Baldwin's "Stranger in the Village"', *The New Yorker*, 19 August 2014.

193 Quoted in Adrian Piper, 'The Triple Negation of Colored Women Artists', *Out of Order, Out of Sight, Volume 2: Selected Writings in Art Criticism, 1967-1992*, Cambridge, MA: The MIT Press, 1996, p.161.

194 'Interview with David Hammons' (conducted by K. Jones), *op. cit.*, pp.255-56.

195 Zora Neale Hurston, 'How It Feels to Be Colored Me', *The World Tomorrow*, May 1928, pp.215-16; reprinted in Julia Reidhead (ed.), *The Norton Anthology of American Literature: 1914-1945*, New York: W.W. Norton, 2012, p.541.

196 Brian O'Doherty, *Inside the White Cube: Ideology of the Exhibition Space*, Los Angeles: University of California Press, 2000, pp.14 and 76.

197 'Interview with David Hammons' (conducted by K. Jones), *op. cit.*, p.251.

198 *Ibid.*, p.255.

199 For more on these projects, see my 'David Hammons, Untitled (Knobkerry), 1994', in E. Filipovic (ed.), *The Artist as Curator: An Anthology*, *op. cit.*, pp.261-81; M. Diawara, 'Dak'Art 2004 Sheep Raffle', *op. cit.*, pp.138-55; and Iolanda Pensa, 'Art and Artists at Dak'Art 2004', *Nafas Art Magazine*, May 2004, available at u-in-u.com/nafas/articles/2004/dakart-2004/ (last accessed on 12 July 2017).

200 B. O'Doherty, *Inside the White Cube*, *op. cit.*, p.80.

201 'You Have to be Prepared: A Conversation Between David Hammons and Robert Storr', *op. cit.*, p.30.

202 *Ibid.*

203 Z. Neale Hurston, 'How It Feels to Be Colored Me', *op. cit.*, p.541.

204 M. Diawara, 'The Blackface Stereotype', in David Levinthal (ed.), *Blackface*, Santa Fe: Arena Editions, 1999, p.7.

205 D. Bey, 'David Hammons: In the Spirit of *Minkisi*', *op. cit.*, p.54.

206 J.B., 'Conversing with David Hammons', *op. cit.*, p.6.

207 Joseph Scanlan, 'David Hammons, Illinois State Museum, Springfield', *Frieze*, no.16, May 1994, p.54.

208 'Deep within the word "American" is its association with race. ... American means white, and Africanist people struggle to make the term applicable to themselves with ethnicity and hyphen after hyphen after hyphen.' Toni Morrison, *Playing in the Dark: Whiteness and the Literary Imagination*, Cambridge, MA: Harvard University Press, 1992, p.47.

209 See Carrie Rickey, 'David Hammons: The New Museum Window', *Artforum*, vol.19, no.2, October 1980, p.80.

210 The line comes from a one-act play by John Farris, and the character of the 'unusual artist' is almost certainly a stand-in for Hammons. See J. Farris, 'Is it Reel or is it Memorex: Out of His Window', *Parkett*, vol.31, March 1992, p.42.

211 'Gerhard Richter: Forty Years of Painting', Museum of Modern Art, New York, 14 February-20 May 2002. Steve Cannon recounted the details of the exhibition in conversation with the author, with the assistance of A. Katsof, New York, 2 July 2015.

212 *Ibid.*

213 I thank Abraham Cruzvillegas, Erma Estwick, A.C. Hudgins, Corrine Jennings and Jeanne Rohatyn Greenberg for describing Hammons's process of making dust drawings.

214 It is noteworthy (and perfectly in keeping with his complex relationship to documentation) that in 2006 Hammons himself commissioned a text by one of the curators about his (non)participation in the biennial, although not for publication, but instead for his 'archives'. The author, Philippe Vergne, eventually published it as 'Miles Away', in Michelle Piranio (ed.), *David Hammons Yves Klein / Yves Klein David Hammons*, Aspen, CO: Aspen Art Museum, 2014, p.105.

215 Anthony Huberman, 'I (Not Love) Information', *Afterall*, issue 16, Autumn/Winter 2007, p.25.

216 Similarly, for the 2016 Marrakech Biennale, Hammons's project was the unlikely prediction of rain on the last day of the biennial (8 May) with no mention of the 'artwork' to appear in any printed or other form. The only clue was two stick-pin brooches representing tiny umbrellas given to the curator and her assistant to wear, barely noticeable unless you knew to look. A Hammons rumour circulated anyway.

217 D. Hammons (as told to David Velasco), '500 Words', *Artforum.com*, 24 November 2008, http://artforum.com/words/id=21506 (last accessed on 12 July 2017).

218 The piece would have been seemed a natural extension of his piece *Bag Lady*, conceived as part of the *Casino Fantasma* exhibition organized by P.S.1 in Venice in 1990, and for which Hammons hung counterfeit designer bags and costume jewelry on an outdoor statue of a naked Venus figure.

219 Fred Wilson and Heather Bursch, email correspondence with the author, 27 May 2018. I thank them for clarifying the rumour.

220 J. Farris, 'Is It Reel or Is It Memorex', *op. cit.*, p.42.

221 D. Bey, conversations with the author, with the assistance of A. Katsof, New York, 17 July 2014 and 22 May 2015. Kerry James Marshall similarly described the surviving snowball, which he witnessed during a visit to JAM with members of the Black Rock Coalition. Conversation with the author, Cologne, 23 January 2014.

222 Goode Bryant recalls Hammons storing some in her home freezer, and that eventually he removed all but one. She also recalls seeing some in Angela Valeria's freezer in Brooklyn. Conversation with the author, with the assistance of A. Katsof, New York, 30 June 2014.

223 See G. Trebay, 'Pole Vault', *op. cit.*, p.73.

224 Recounted in conversations with the author, with the assistance of A. Katsof, by: Arthur Jafa, 15 September 2015; Vernon Reid, 5 August 2014; Greg Tate, 25 July 2014; and L. Goode Bryant, 26 June 2014, 30 June 2015 and 2 October 2015. Brian Wolff, the neighbouring photographer, summed up the sentiment of the event: 'I hardly remember my name but remember rescuing the snowball! You don't have many opportunities to be a hero!' Conversation with the author, with the assistance of A. Katsof, New York, 27 June 2014.

225 D. Hammons, telephone conversation with the author, 21 August 2014.

226 As Price astutely argues: 'The power of the readymade is that no one needs to make the pilgrimage to see *Fountain*. As with [Dan] Graham's magazine pieces, few people saw the original *Fountain* in 1917. Never exhibited, and lost or destroyed almost immediately, it was actually created through Duchamp's media manipulations. ... Distribution is a circuit of reading, and there is huge potential for subversion when dealing with the institutions that control definitions of cultural meaning.' S. Price, *Dispersion*, *op. cit.*

227 D. Hammons, quoted in D. Menaker Rothschild, 'Reflections of a Long Distance Runner', *op. cit.*, pp.51-52.

228 From the fax on display at Mnuchin Gallery, New York in the exhibition 'David Hammons: Five Decades'.

229 Adam Sheffer, telephone conversation with the author, 15 July 2016.

230 D. Hammons, quoted in D. Menaker Rothschild, 'Reflections of a Long Distance Runner', *op. cit.*, p.46.

231 The curiously little serious research on the event testifies to this.

232 D. Hammons, telephone conversation with the author, 22 August 2014.

233 *Ibid.*

234 D. Hammons, conversation with the author, New York, 29 September 2015.